POLISH WINGS

Adam Gołąbek

MiG-29
1989-2009

First 20 years in PAF
part one

STRATUS

Polish Wings

Wydawnictwo STRATUS s.c.
Po. Box 123, 27-600 Sandomierz 1, Poland
phone. 0-15 833 30 41
e-mail: office@stratusbooks.pl
www.stratusbooks.com.pl www.mmpbooks.biz

Copyright© 2010 Stratus

ISBN 978-83-61421-06-1

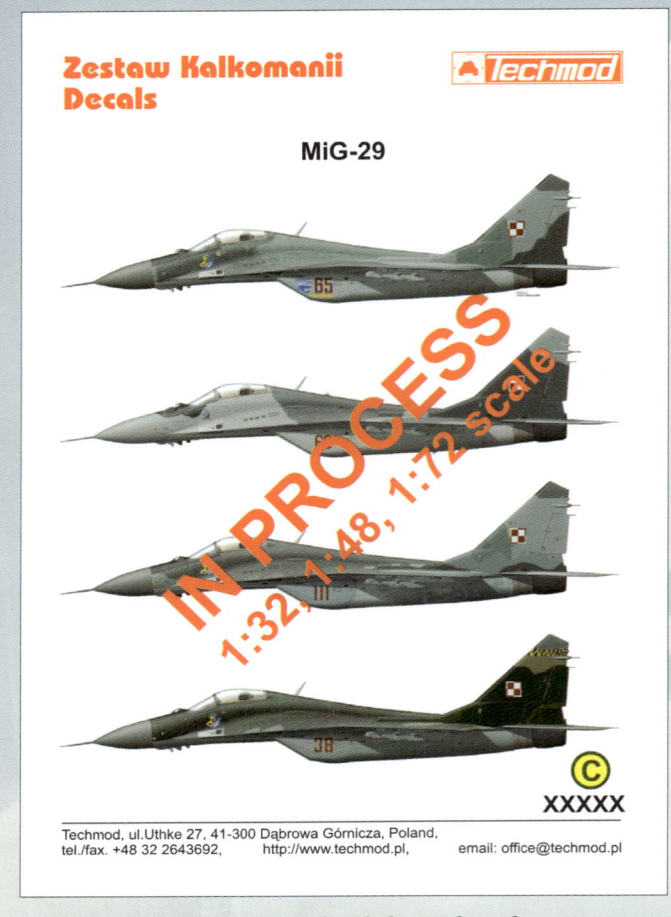

All rights reserved. Apart from any fair dealing for the purpose of private study, research, criticism or review, as permitted under the Copyright, Design and Patents Act, 1988, no part of this publication may be reproduced, stored in a retrieval system, or transmitted in any form or by any means, electronic, electrical, chemical, mechanical, optical, photocopying, recording or otherwise, without prior written permission. All enquiries should be addressed to the publisher.

Photo credit:
Adam Gołąbek (201), Robert Cierniak (1), Grzegorz Czubski (2), Wacław Hołyś (2), Andrzej Rogucki (23), Norbert Czajkowski (2), Rafał Tokarski (5), Robert Gretzyngier (3), Wojtek Matusiak (5), Marian Karpiel (1), Andrzej Krzewski (5).

Layout concept	Bartłomiej Belcarz
	Artur Bukowski
Cover concept	Artur Juszczak
Cover	Marek Ryś
Translation	Wojtek Matusiak
DTP	Artur Bukowski,
	Bartłomiej Belcarz
Colour Drawings	Marek Radomski
Edited by	Roger Wallsgrove

Wydawnictwo Diecezjalne i Drukarnia w Sandomierzu
ul. Żeromskiego 4, 27-600 Sandomierz, Poland
phone: +48 15 644 04 00
PRINTED IN POLAND

Media partner in Poland:

Wydawnictwo Sanko ul. Jastrzębia 13/6, 53-148 Wrocław
(0 71) 338 42 89, e-mail: magazyn@sanko.wroclaw.pl

TECHMOD, ul. Uthke 27, 41-300 Dąbrowa Górnicza
(0 32) 264 36 92, e-mail: techmod@techmod.com.pl

Forthcoming decals by Techmod.
Techmod will release decals for the MiG-29 based on the information, photos and profiles published in this book.
Decals will be available separately.

AVAILABLE

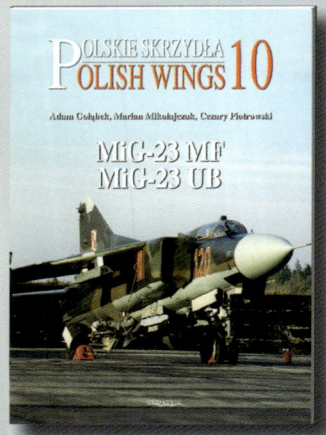

Polskie Skrzydła / Polish Wings 10 — MiG-23 MF / MiG-23 UB

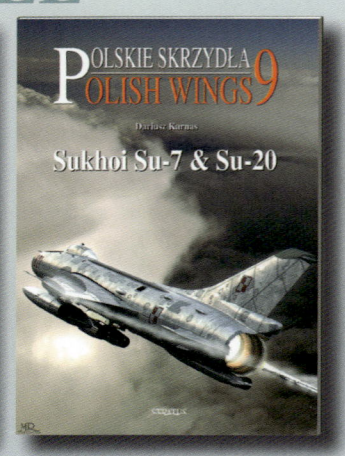

Polskie Skrzydła / Polish Wings 9 — Sukhoi Su-7 & Su-20

FORTHCOMING

Polskie Skrzydła / Polish Wings 5 — Ex USAAF Aircraft 1945

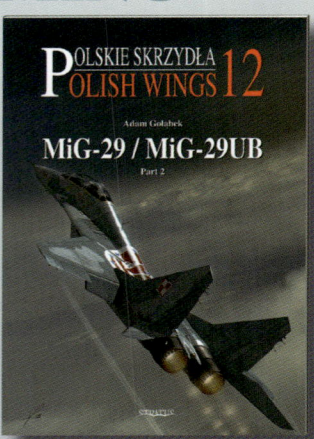

Polskie Skrzydła / Polish Wings 12 — MiG-29 / MiG-29UB Part 2

Polskie Skrzydła

MIKOYAN MiG-29

The MiG-29 is currently the only Russian-built, air-superiority fighter in Polish Air Force service. It is also the only Russian-built fighter in service with some NATO countries. During the late 1980s and early 1990s it replaced the worn and increasingly obsolete MiG-21 (NATO codename 'Fishbed') as well as the slightly younger MiG-23 ('Flogger'). The new fighter was to be the counterpart of the American F-16 "Fighting Falcon", then entering service with NATO.

Initial negotiations regarding procurement of the new aircraft for the Polish Air Force took place on 23-26 October 1985. The Polish delegation, under the Head of Aircraft Technology, Gen. Mieczysław Sikorski, was invited to Moscow, and then visited Kubinka air base, where a presentation had been prepared. During the meeting the Polish side defined their needs: at least 36 combat aircraft and 6 trainers. The new aircraft were going to arrive in Poland by the end of 1995, to equip three fighter regiments.

In July 1987 the Polish MoD placed an official order for nine aircraft of the 9-12A version and three 9-51A combat trainers. After documentation was supplied, the contract was signed in March 1989. Delivery of MiG-29s to Poland was due, so in the autumn of 1988 a group of 20 pilots was selected from the 1. *PLM* (1. *Pułk Lotnictwa Myśliwskiego* – 1st Fighter Aviation Regiment), to undergo initial selection for conversion training on the new aircraft type. None of them was aware what type they were going to fly in the future. The data available to them at the time said that the selected personnel would be trained on "high manoeuvrability aircraft".

The selection was very strict. Doctors selected those candidates who were able to endure an 8g force for 30 seconds. After subsequent tests 12 top pilots were selected: *płk* Jerzy Pacześniak, *ppłk* Zenon Kida, *mjr* Ryszard Bruździak, *mjr* Czesław Ciodyk, *kpt*. Ireneusz Piasecki, *por*. Zdzisław Lackowski, *kpt*. Kazimierz Michalik, *por*. Henryk Chołuj, *por*. Waldemar Łubowski, *kpt*. Marian Zięba, *por*. Wiesław Rec and *por*. Jacek Wojtaszczyk. On 28 February 1989 a Soviet Il-18 transport aircraft took the selected pilots and ground personnel to Frunze in the USSR (now in Kyrgyzstan).

Several months before, air and ground training had been completed there by Indian and Rumanian Air Force personnel. A group of Czechoslovak pilots and technicians were undergoing training at the same time as the Polish team. The regiment there had a total of some 18 MiG-23s and 38 MiG-29s that allowed smooth training for everybody. According to the accounts of the trainee pilots all aircraft were very well maintained and despite high daily numbers of flying hours faults or failures were rare and mostly minor.

Final exams of the theoretical course took place on 23-28 March, after which flying training commenced on MiG-29UB two-seat combat trainers. Four local instructors started to train the Polish pilots, each of the tutors being in charge of three Poles.

First flights took place at 6 o'clock on 12 April 1989. The initial take-offs were to acquaint the Polish pilots both with the aircraft and the flying sector. After two days of dual-control flying they started to go solo. According to the contract each of the trainee pilots was going to accumulate 15 flying hours in the subsequent stages of training: local flying, medium and low altitude flying, pair flying, interceptions, and ground attack training on a firing range. In the final stage the pilots made stratospheric flights.

Flying usually commenced early in the morning and continued until almost noon, when it was interrupted due to high

[1]: MiG-29 in flight at high altitude, 2007.

Polish Wings

temperatures. Then, after several hours break and a meal pilots resumed flying, which ended late in the evening. The Polish pilots suffered from illnesses due to the difficult climate, and Soviet doctors often declared them unfit for flying.

Training was completed by 26 May. The pilots achieved the required level of skills to continue further training in their home country. Five pilots, Ryszard Bruździak, Czesław Ciodyk, Marian Zięba, Jacek Wojtaszczyk and Zenon Kida completed extra flying hours and theoretical training and passed exams to obtain instructors' certificates.

The extra flying time was accumulated, in part, during an exercise of the Soviet forces that took place at the same time as the Polish and Czechoslovak teams trained.

After a Soviet pilot defected in a MiG-29 to Turkey, engineering services practiced closing the airfield during flying training by placing support vehicles across the runway. The pilots themselves had to stop their aircraft in predefined places during taxiing, take-off or landing to block the runway. This led to some confusing or even dangerous situations at the airfield. But these were not the only problems encountered during the course.

Language problems were frequent during flying, as were troubles caused by a different approach of the Soviets to the training sorties of Polish pilots. In the regiments of the Polish Air Force it was customary that if the task was accomplished in a shorter time than originally planned then, fuel and free airspace permitting, the task could be repeated or another one performed. The Soviets, however, considered such behaviour a flying offence and their instructors insisted on suspending or even termination of training of the 'undisciplined' pilots. Fortunately, the matter could be explained and no pilots were banned. On 1 June the entire Polish team returned to Poland by air.

The first MiG-29s were delivered to Poland in late July 1989. These were four single-seaters, serial nos. 2960526365, 2960526366, 2960526367, and 2960526370.

The aircraft were delivered by Soviet pilots who then handed them over officially to the Polish side at Mińsk Mazowiecki air base. All the machines featured maintenance stencilling in Russian. They had no national markings or code numbers, and these were applied after acceptance inspection of the new MiGs.

[2]: Pre-flight check of '83' before a flight to a training range, 2007.
[3]: '108' taking off from Dęblin air base, 2005.
[4]: '108' taxiing to the apron, 2006.

Polskie Skrzydła

Code numbers were applied to individual aircraft according to the same rule as with other types used by the Polish Air Force: each aircraft displayed the last two, later three, digits of the serial number.

The next three aircraft were delivered on 1 August 1989. These were two-seat trainers, serial nos. N50903014615, N50903014642 and N50903014664. All the aircraft were allocated to the first flight of the 1. *PLM*, its MiG-21s going to the second flight. The two-seaters received code numbers from the last two digits of their respective serial numbers.

First flights on the new aircraft were performed on 9 August. The pilots trained in the USSR carried out their first solo flights in Poland.

The last five aircraft from the contract were taken on charge on 2 October 1990. These were serial nos. 2960535105, 2960535108, 2960535111, 2960535114 and 2960535115. Their code numbers consisted of the last three digits of the respective serial numbers. Thus the regiment at Mińsk Mazowiecki had nine single-seat fighters (9-12A version) and three two-seat combat trainers (9-51A).

More Polish pilots achieved combat readiness after 18 months of training in Poland, and MiG-29s were first on combat alert duty at Mińsk Mazowiecki on 13 January 1992. However, already in June 1990 the experienced pilots flew their first training sorties using B–8 unguided missile launchers and 50 to 250 kg bombs. This was also an opportunity to train more pilots in this kind of operations. Less than a year later, in early May, pilots completed their first air-to-air missile firing sorties over the sea range at Wicko Morskie.

[5]: A MiG-29 armed with R-73 missiles taxiing at sunset, 2008.
[6]: MiG-29 '115' ready for a night sortie, 2007.

Polish Wings

No further procurements from Russia followed, despite the ambitious original plans. It had been planned to purchase some 110 aircraft of the type, to replace all the MiG-21s (PFM, M, MF, and eventually the latest 'bis' variants) by the end of 1998.

In 1995 it became possible to acquire MiG-29s formerly used by the Czech Air Force. The contract was for nine single-seat and one two-seat aircraft with spares and armament in exchange for eleven brand new Polish PZL *Sokół* helicopters with additional equipment. Despite some criticism, the transaction proved a success. Despite several years of operation the aircraft were in very good condition. Additionally, all the aircraft had been withdrawn from use and properly stored.

The first five ex-Czech aircraft, serial nos. 2960532038, 2960532359, 2960526377, 2960526392 (single-seaters) and N50903014528 (trainer) landed at the snow-covered Mińsk Mazowiecki air base on 22 December 1995. The next machine, no. 2960526386, landed seven days later, and was the last one delivered before the end of the year.

The last four aircraft, nos. 2960532040, 2960532054, 2960532056 and 2960526383, were delivered on 8 January 1996.

All the aircraft delivered from the Czech Republic were easily distinguished from those obtained directly from the USSR during 1989-90. They were finished in a darker camouflage scheme of different colours and carried four-digit code numbers on their fins. It was decided that until a major overhaul the aircraft would not be repainted. Only the Czech markings were going to be replaced with Polish ones and the code numbers changed according to the Polish standard. The latter would be reapplied on the sides of the air intakes and abbreviated to the last two digits of the serial number, in line with other Polish MiGs.

As expected, the ex-Czech aircraft were allocated to the 2nd flight of the 1. *PLM*, which allowed withdrawal of the last MiG-21Ms, 33 years after the 'Fishbed' was first introduced in the unit.

On 19 February 1996 all the ex-Czech machines were officially handed over to the 1. *PLM* by the Chief of the General Staff, gen. Tadeusz Wilecki.

MiG-29 colours

Although the MiG-29 was introduced into service at the time of a booming tendency to apply regimental and flight badges, the type did not see many spectacular schemes. During 20 years of operation with the Polish Air Force the type has displayed just a few unit badges and a few personal emblems. Individual aircraft bore occasional special or personal markings, and certain machines had interesting and attractive markings. The camouflage colours did not differ between aircraft, with a few exceptions. The situation changed after the ex-Czech, and then ex-German, machines were introduced into service.

The initial MiG-29s introduced into service with the 1. *PLM* featured the original factory-applied camouflage scheme, no different from that on aircraft built and used in the USSR. The scheme consisted of two colours: light grey on lower and upper surfaces of the aircraft and areas of darker grey on upper surfaces and fins. All aircraft had radomes and fin tips in dark grey.

A black anti-glare panel was applied forward of the windscreen. Code numbers and maintenance stencilling were in red.

The camouflage was applied with semi-matt paints. All the aircraft delivered to Poland had the same general pattern, with the sole exception of no. 67, which featured a different pattern on the fuselage, wings and fins, while retaining the same

Scheme name	Description	Camouflage and colours	Remarks
Czech	Aircraft delivered in Czech camouflage colours	Four shades of green and brown on uppersurfaces as follows: Dark Olive-green – FS 34079 Light Green – FS 34227 Light Brown – FS 30227 Dark Brown – FS 30045 Light Grey-blue – FS 36495 on undersurfaces. Aircraft have same general pattern with sole exception of no. 67 which featured a completely different pattern. Nose radome, panels on LERX and spine as well as vertical tails in Dark Grey – FS 36118. Black anti-glare panel. Gun vent and leading edge of horizontal tailplanes were left unpainted	Aircraft were used in this camouflage between December 1995 and January 2002.
Russian delivery	Russian factory-applied camouflage scheme.	Two colours as follows: Upper and undersurfaces - Light Grey – FS 36495 Uppersurfaces - Grey – FS 36329 Each aircraft has individual camouflage pattern. Nose radome, panels on both sides of LERX, panel on top of spine, top parts of vertical tails were painted in Medium Grey Black anti-glare panel. Gun vent and leading edge of horizontal tailplanes were left unpainted	Aircraft were used in this camouflage between July 1989 and October 2002.
WZL-2 (overhaul) 1st period	Aircraft after overhaul at WZL-2 in Bydgoszcz (December 1997-April 2007)	Three colours as follows: Light grey – FS 36270 and Dark Grey – FS 36118 on uppersurfaces Blue-grey/Light Grey – FS 36375 on undersurfaces Each aircraft has individual camouflage pattern. Black anti-glare panel.	Aircraft were used in this camouflage since December 1997.
WZL-2 (overhaul) 2nd period	Aircraft after the second overhaul at WZL-2 in Bydgoszcz. Since April 2007	Three colours as follows: Light grey – FS 36270 and Dark Grey – FS 36118 on uppersurfaces Blue-grey/Light grey – FS 36375 on undersurfaces Each aircraft has individual camouflage pattern. Black anti-glare panel.	Aircraft in this camouflage since April 2007.

Polskie Skrzydła

[7]: '83' taking off from Mińsk Mazowiecki to practice the aerobatic routine before an air display in Finland. Mjr pil. Artur Kałko is at the controls.
[8]: '105' moments after take-off. UZR-73 training missile can be seen under the wing, 2007
[9]: A MiG-29 about to touch down at Mińsk Mazowiecki, 2008.
[10]: Aircraft being prepared for flying. Main apron at Mińsk Mazowiecki, 2007.
[11]: '83' completes a sortie at sunset, 2008.

Polish Wings

[12]: A pair scramble during 'Fruit Fly' exercise, 2007.
[13]: '114' prepared for ground testing, 2007.
[14]: '40' at Mińsk Mazowiecki, 2006.
[15]: '83' taxiing with the brake parachute still deployed, 2007.

Polskie Skrzydła

	Code no.	Serial no.	Czech AF code no.	Unit allocations			Camouflage scheme	Notes
1	38	2960532038	3810	22.12.1995 31.12.1998 23.02.2000 01.01.2001 07.07.2007 24.07.2009	- 31.12.1998 - 22.02.2000 - 01.01.2001 - 07.07.2006 - 24.07.2009	- 1.PLM - WZL-2 - 1.PLM - 1.elt - WZL-2 - 1.elt	Czech scheme Post-overhaul scheme (1st period) Post-overhaul scheme (2nd period)	On 20 January 2006 the cockpit canopy fell off immediately after take-off. The pilot *por.* Grzegorz Czubka landed safely on the airfield after using the necessary fuel. The machine was repaired and returned to service. On 24 July 2009 the aircraft was flown back after the 2nd overhaul by *kpt.* Tadeusz Grzeszuk. (See page 14)
2	40	2960532040	4012	08.01.1996 13.10.1999 17.08.2001 11.12.2009	- 13.10.1999 - 17.08.2001 - 11.12.2009	- 1.PLM - WZL-2 - 1.elt - WZL-2	Czech scheme Post-overhaul scheme (1st period)	Took part in PKW 'Orlik' mission in 2006. Currently undergoing 2nd major overhaul (See page 22).
3	54	2960532354	5414	08.01.1996 01.01.2001 06.04.2001 19.12.2003 18.11.2009	- 01.01.2001 - 05.04.2001 - 11.12.2003 - 18.11.2009	- 1.PLM - 1.elt - WZL-2 - 1.elt - WZL-2	Czech scheme Post-overhaul scheme (1st period)	Took part in PKW 'Orlik' mission in 2006. Currently undergoing 2nd major overhaul (See page 24) .
4	56	2960532356	5616	08.01.1996 26.01.1999 11.04.2000 23.04.2008 20.11.2009	- 26.01.1999 - 11.04.2000 - 23.04.2008 - 20.11.2009	- 1.PLM - WZL-2 - 1.elt - WZL-2 - 1.elt	Czech scheme Post-overhaul scheme (1st period) Post-overhaul scheme (2nd period)	Took part in PKW 'Orlik' mission in 2006 as backup aircraft. After 2nd major overhaul (See page 28).
5	59	2960532359	5918	22.12.1995 26.01.1999 31.07.2000 01.01.2001 07.08.2008	- 25.01.1999 - 31.07.2000 - 01.01.2001 - 07.08.2008	- 1.PLM - WZL-2 - 1.PLM - 1.elt - WZL-2	Czech scheme Post-overhaul scheme (1st period)	On 17 October 2000 suffered hydraulics failure during flight. The emergency landing ended in the ATU-2M (emergency arresting barrier). The aircraft was repaired and returned to service. (See page 32)
6	65	2960526365	-	21.07.1989 08.02.1998 18.05.1999 01.01.2001 19.03.2007 12.12.2008 12.12.2008	- 05.02.1998 - 18.05.1999 - 01.01.2001 - 19.03.2007 - 12.12.2008 - 12.12.2008	- 1.PLM - WZL-2 - 1.PLM - 1.elt - WZL-2 - 1.elt - 41.elt	Russian delivery scheme Post-overhaul scheme (1st period) Post-overhaul scheme (2nd period)	Flown to Malbork from *WZL-2* after the 2nd overhaul on 17 December 2008. Failure during reception tests. Planned to be collected by 1.*elt* and formally allocated to that unit. Eventually collected by 41.*elt* and flown to Malbork on 17 December 2008. (See page 35)
7	66	2960526366	-	17.07.1989 26.06.1997 18.01.1999 01.01.2001 07.12.2006 22.02.2008	- 26.06.1997 - 18.01.1999 - 01.01.2001 - 07.12.2006 - 22.02.2008	- 1.PLM - WZL-2 - 1.PLM - 1.elt - WZL-2 - 41.elt	Russian delivery scheme Post-overhaul scheme (1st period) Post-overhaul scheme (2nd period)	On 4 September 2001 suffered hydraulics failure during flight. The damaged aircraft flown by *kpt.* Robert Kozak landed with one main wheel down. The aircraft swung off the runway and stopped in the grass. It was repaired and returned to service. Allocated to 41.*elt* and flown to Malbork from *WZL-2* on 25 February 2008. (See page 38)
8	67	2960526367	-	17.07.1989 31.03.2000 21.03.2002 23.04.2009	- 31.03.2000 - 14.02.2002 - 23.04.2009	- 1.FLM - WZL-2 - 1.elt - WZL-2	Russian delivery scheme Post-overhaul scheme (1st period)	Currently undergoing 2nd major overhaul. (See page 41)
9	70	2960526370	-	14.07.1989 ??.12.1996 15.12.1997 01.01.2001 06.01.2006 26.04.2007	-??.12.1996 -15.12.1997 -01.01.2001 -06.01.2006 -26.04.2007	- 1. PLM - WZL - 2 - 1. PLM - 1. elt - WZL - 2 - 41.elt	Russian delivery scheme Post-overhaul scheme (1st period) Post-overhaul scheme (2nd period)	Planned to be collected by 1.*elt* and formally allocated to that unit. Retained at *WZL-2* for technical reasons and eventually allocated to 41.*elt*. Flown to Malbork on 26 April 2008. (See page 46)
10	77	2960526377	7702	22.12.1995 31.12.1998 18.10.1999 01.01.2001 08.08.2007 22.12.2008 22.12.2008	- 31.12.1998 - 18.10.1999 - 01.01.2001 - 08.08.2007 - 22.12.2008 - 22.12.2008	- 1.PLM - WZL-2 - 1.PLM - 1.elt - WZL-2 - 1.elt - 41.elt	Czech scheme Post-overhaul scheme (1st period) Post-overhaul scheme (2nd period)	When returning from a deployment to Malbork, the aircraft approached to land at their home base at Mińsk Mazowiecki. They encountered an extensive storm cloud north-east of the base. The MiG-29 flown by Adam Rogalski flew across the cloud and landed. '77' flown by *kpt. pil.* Tomasz Jatczak entered the cloud and was struck by ball lightning which entered the cockpit. The machine showed no damage and the pilot landed safely at the base. A subsequent inspection revealed damaged electric cables and avionics systems. The machine was repaired and returned to service. Planned to be collected by 1.*elt* and formally allocated to that unit. Eventually collected by 41.*elt* and flown to Malbork from *WZL-2* on 13 January 2009. (See page 50)
11	83	2960526383	8304	08.01.1996 01.01.2001 02.01.2002 21.01.2003 26.06.2009	- 01.01.2001 - 01.01.2002 - 20.12.2002 - 26.06.2009	- 1.PLM - 1.elt - WZL-2 - 1.elt - WZL-2	Czech scheme Post-overhaul scheme (1st period)	Featured white bands on the rear fuselage/fins for the 'Eagle's Talon '97' exercise. (See page 54)
12	89	2960526389	8906	29.12.1995 10.07.1999 04.12.2000 01.01.2001 13.10.2008	- 10.07.1999 - 04.12.2000 - 01.01.2001 - 13.10.2008	- 1.PLM - WZL-2 - 1.PLM - 1.elt - WZL-2	Czech scheme Post-overhaul scheme (1st period)	Featured white bands on the rear fuselage/fins for the 'Eagle's Talon '97' exercise. (See page 58).
13	92	2960526392	9207	22.12.1995 31.12.1998 21.05.1999 01.01.2001 05.12.2006 05.03.2008	- 31.12.1998 - 20.05.1999 - 01.01.2001 - 05.12.2006 - 05.03.2008	- 1.PLM - WZL-2 - 1.PLM - 1.elt - WZL-2 - 41.elt	Czech scheme Post-overhaul scheme (1st period) Post-overhaul scheme (2nd period)	Featured white bands on the rear fuselage/fins for the 'Eagle's Talon '97' exercise. (See page 61)
14	105	2960535105	-	02.10.1990 01.01.2001 28.09.2002 04.02.2005	- 01.01.2001 - 27.09.2002 - 04.02.2005	- 1.PLM - 1.elt - WZL-2 - 1.elt	Russian delivery scheme Post-overhaul scheme (1st period)	Tested in Israel in 1997 (test centre at Negev desert) (See page 65).
15	108	2960535108	-	02.10.1990 01.01.2001 07.09.2002 29.12.2004	- 01.01.2001 - 06.09.2002 - 29.12.2004	- 1.PLM - 1.elt - WZL-2 - 1.elt	Russian delivery scheme Post-overhaul scheme (1st period)	**(See page 71)**
16	111	2960535111	-	02.10.1990 09.09.2000 09.06.2003	- 08.09.2000 - 04.06.2003	- 1.PLM - WZL-2 - 1.elt	Russian delivery scheme Post-overhaul scheme (1st period)	Took part in PKW 'Orlik' mission in 2006. (See page 76)
17	114	2960535114	-	02.10.1990 01.01.2001 27.09.2002 12.05.2005	- 01.01.2001 - 27.09.2002 - 12.05.2005	- 1.PLM - 1.elt - WZL-2 - 1.elt	Russian delivery scheme Post-overhaul scheme (1st period)	Tested in Israel in 1997 (test centre at Negev desert). Featured white bands on the rear fuselage/fins for the 'Eagle's Talon '97' exercise. (See page 81)
18	115	2960535115	-	02.10.1990 01.01.2001 07.11.2002 27.07.2005	- 01.01.2001 - 22.10.2002 - 27.07.2005	- 1.PLM - 1.elt - WZL-2 - 1.elt	Russian delivery scheme Post-overhaul scheme (1st period)	Tested in Israel in 1997 (test centre at Negev desert). Took part in PKW 'Orlik' mission in 2006. (See page 85)

Polish Wings

colours. Also the two-seat trainers featured a different pattern but with the same colours (MiG-29UB are described in part 2).

During operation the finish would gradually wear down. It was retouched by the maintenance flight using available paints. The repainted area was proportional to the amount of damage to the airframe's surface, often eventually resulting in a new camouflage pattern. New paint was most often applied around the cockpit, inspection panels, cockpit entry ladder support, radome and its joint with the fuselage, and on leading edges of the wings and tail surfaces.

This was the situation until December 1995/January 1996, when the ex-Czech aircraft were delivered to Mińsk Mazowiecki.

The aircraft from the Czech Republic retained their camouflage of several shades of green and brown. All these aircraft still had some flying time left prior to major overhaul, and to save cost the painting scheme was left unchanged. However, to get the ex-Czech aircraft flying it was necessary, apart from thorough inspection, to replace all the national markings, to overpaint the old codes on the fins and reapply Polish ones on air intake sides, and to overpaint the emblems of the previous operator, the 1st 'Tiger' Regiment from Žatec. This was done with semi-matt green paint (identical in structure and characteristics to that used on Polish aircraft) similar in colour to those used by the Czechs. Apart from their conspicuous camouflage, the ex-Czech aircraft were also distinctive in having the 'tiger' motif at the top of fin outer surfaces.

In late April/early May 1997 by arrangement with Israel three Polish aircraft, code nos. 105, 114 and 115, went to the secret test centre in the Negev desert.

Upon the move all Polish markings and emblems were overpainted with grey paint. The emblem of the Israeli Flight Test Centre was applied at the top of the fins. The aircraft continued to fly in this guise for about two weeks, and were then prepared for the move back to Poland. This involved removing the Israeli emblems and reapplying Polish national markings on the wings and fins. The aircraft returned to Poland in such livery.

A few weeks after their return the machines had the 1. *PLM* emblems reapplied. All three aircraft retained traces of the 'Israeli episode' in the form of distinctive patches on the fins where the Israeli emblems have been overpainted and grey patches under the reapplied Polish markings and regimental badges. In such guise they then continued to fly (with subsequent minor retouching) until their major overhauls.

Major overhauls of Polish MiG-29s commenced in early 1997. Aircraft no. 70 was the first to undergo overhaul, which included complete replacement of the paint coat. *WZL-2* (Wojskowe Zakłady Lotnicze nr 2, No. 2 Military Aircraft Works) at Bydgoszcz had developed a new paint scheme of three colours: blue-grey/light grey (FS 36375) on lower surfaces, and areas of light grey (FS 36270) and dark grey (FS 36118) on upper surfaces.

In 1993 new regulations appeared, changing the national markings of the Polish military aviation. The arrangement of red and white fields in the checkerboard was altered, by turning the checkerboard through 90°. These new markings were applied on all new planes; on planes currently in service the markings were changed successively, mainly during overhauls. The process of change took a few years.

A black anti-glare panel in front of the windscreen was added by the regiment. Similar black panels were applied by the regiment on subsequent aircraft, code nos. 65, 66, 92, 77 (the latter later received a small black retouch around the IFF aerial fitted forward of the windscreen) and 15 (two-seat trainer), that did not receive these upon overhaul. The black anti-glare panel was first applied at the overhaul facility on aircraft nos. 38 and 28.

All paints used on the aircraft were matt and of very good quality, and this guaranteed retaining the same colour and uniform structure on the airframe. As opposed to the aircraft in factory-applied finish the radome was included in the new scheme and painted with the same paints as the rest of the aircraft. The new scheme has remained unchanged until

[16]: '108' taking off from Mińsk Mazowiecki, 2008.

Polskie Skrzydła

the present day. All aircraft undergoing overhauls have then been repainted in the three-tone camouflage with matt paints, and since mid-2002 with semi-matt finishes. This also applies to the ex-German aircraft overhauled at *WZL-2* (Ex-German MiG-29s are described in part 2).

It is worth noting here that the scheme prepared in late 1997 only applied to colours used in the post-overhaul camouflage.

Additionally, radomes have repeatedly been switched between aircraft during routine maintenance and post-flight servicing. This is easy to spot when the pattern on the radome does not fit the nose colours at the joint. For example, aircraft nos. 40, 83 and 115 in the new camouflage were fitted with radomes from other machines undergoing routine maintenance.

From the very beginning all aircraft of the 1. *PLM*'s 1st flight were adorned with the unit emblem, the 'Warsaw Mermaid' in yellow. This was applied on both sides zof the fuselage immediately below the cockpit on both the aircraft delivered from the USSR and those acquired from the Czech Republic. The emblem was not applied immediately, however, so some aircraft were flown after inspections and overhauls with the badge on one side only, or no badge at all. Depending on the time of application, the wave at the base was blue on some 'Mermaids' and navy blue on others.

The 1st flight of the regiment was organised in two sections. The first section did not have an emblem, but the second section had a small badge in the form of a bird holding a rocket missile in its claws. This badge was applied on all aircraft of the section, nos. 67, 70, 105, 108 and 111.

In 1991 the code number of aircraft no. 70 was adorned with a circle of stars and the word 'WARSAW' to symbolise the 70th anniversary of the pre-war 1st Air Regiment in Warsaw. However, the special markings did not last long, a few months at most.

Three years later the upper surface of aircraft no. 115 was given one of the most striking artworks on Polish MiG-29s. To commemorate the cooperation between 1. *PLM* and the 2e *Escadre de Chasse* of the French *Armee de l'Air*, based at Dijon, a huge emblem of the French unit, combining the WWI-vintage badges of GC I/2 flights (SPA 3 and SPA 103). Another form of this badge was applied on the fins of MiG-29 no. 115. The aircraft continued to fly in this scheme until April 1997, when it

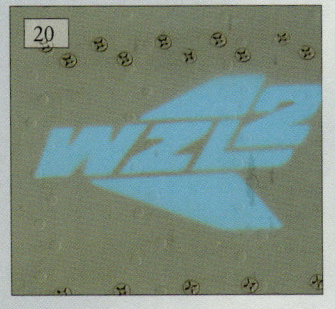

[17]: '70' during morning pre-flight preparations at Malbork.
[18, 19]: Old style emblem of WZL-2 (Wojskowe Zakłady Lotnicze nr 2, No. 2 Military Aircraft Works) at Bydgoszcz applied on aircraft following overhauls, 2000.
[20, 21]: New style emblem of WZL-2, 2005.

Polish Wings

went to Israel and the artwork was overpainted. Notably, upon return to Poland the paint started to peel off and eventually, just prior to the overhaul in late 2002, the artwork was visible again on top of the aircraft, although in a rather sorry state.

In 1995 'Skrzydlata Polska' ('Winged Poland') aviation monthly celebrated its 65th anniversary. To commemorate it MiG no. 65 had the name of the magazine applied in blue near the code numbers on the sides of the air intakes, complemented with 'signs of the time' in the form of silhouettes of aircraft: the pre-WWII RWD light sports aeroplane on the port side and the MiG-29 on the starboard side, with yellow 'trails' behind.

In 1997 an international exercise code named 'Eagle's Talon' was organised in Poland. All participating MiG-29s from the 1. *PLM* (nos. 64, 83, 89 and 114) were marked with a broad white band on the rear fuselage, a quick recognition marking of one of the 'fighting sides'. Following the exercise the bands were overpainted, leaving a prominent mark on the camouflage pattern of each machine.

In 2001, under the general reorganisation of the Polish Air Force, the flying component of the 1. *PLM* was reformed into the 1. *elt* (1. *Eskadra Lotnictwa Taktycznego*, 1st Tactical Fighter Squadron). On most aircraft the '1 *plm*' was removed from the wave motif under the 'Mermaid' badge. However, some aircraft continued to fly with unchanged emblems until as late as 2007 (nos. 15, 38 and 56).

In 2004 aircraft of the 1. *elt* started to be adorned with the old badge dating back to the 'Kosciuszko' Squadron of the 1920 Polish-Russian war. The same badge was used by the 111th Fighter Flight until 1939 and then by 303 Squadron in Britain during WWII. The badge had been accepted as the emblem of the 1st flight in the 1. *PLM*, and then inherited by the 1. *elt*. Its application on aircraft was first suggested by *kpt. pil.* Tomasz Jatczak. The badge was applied on the port side of the fuselage, and on some aircraft it appeared alongside the 'Mermaid' emblem (for example, aircraft no. 15 before and after its 2nd overhaul and no. 56 before its 2nd overhaul).

When MiG-29s were introduced in the 41. *elt* at Malbork, the type was also adorned with emblems inherited from the former MiG-21-equipped 41. *PLM*. An image of a knight against a MiG-21 silhouette was applied on both sides of the aircraft below the windscreen. In 2006 armourers started to apply the 'Toruń Duck' (traditional badge of the Toruń-based fighter units before WWII and of 306 'City of Toruń' Squadron that operated from Britain during the war) on the port air intake aft of the code number. Some aircraft were adorned with symbols of R-60 and R-73 missiles fired during exercises over the sea range at Ustks. On some aircraft more symbols were added above these during May 2007. The new ones displayed missiles and bombs fired and dropped during exercises at Jagodne range. The aircraft that participated in these exercises were adorned with an emblem on the fin that included the name 'Jagodne 07' and a bomb symbol.

Back in 2006 a decal of a knight mounted on a MiG-29 was applied on the aircraft no. 4122. The decal was prepared specially for the annual Commanders' Fly-In at Dęblin, but this was the back-up machine. Eventually the aircraft 'No. 1' was used during the event and the back-up with the artwork on the port side of the radome was not seen in public. The emblem remained on the aircraft until September 2007, when it was removed during a major inspection.

2006 saw the beginning of *PKW* (*Polski Kontyngent Wojskowy*, Polish Military Contingent) '*Orlik*' ('Eaglet'). Four MiGs from the 1. *elt* from Mińsk Mazowiecki were deployed to a base in Lithuania for Baltic Air Policing duties. Aircraft nos. 40, 77, 111 and 115 received the emblem of the mission at the base of their fins. Also MiG no. 56 was based initially in Lithuania, but it was sent back to Poland for routine maintenance inspection

[22]: *41. elt aircraft during landing run at Malbork, 2008.*

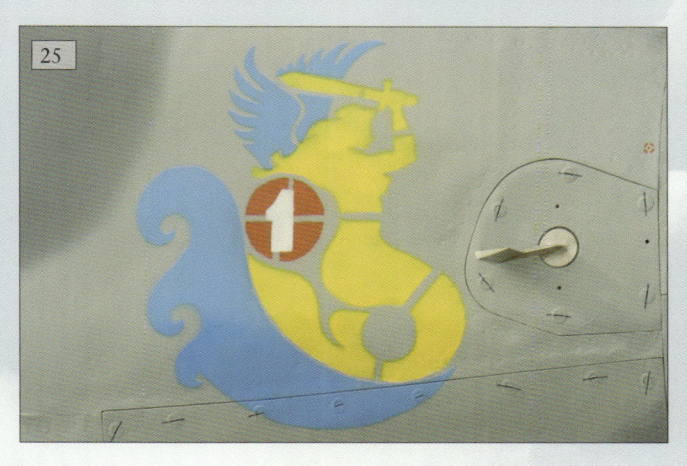

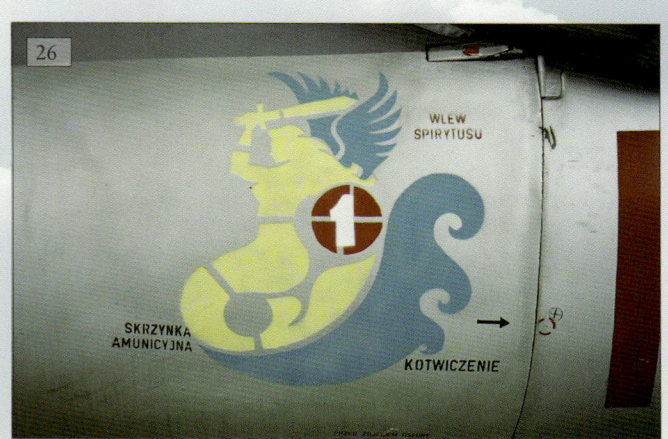

before the emblems were applied on the machines. Three of the aircraft received personal emblems of their pilots: no. 77 with an eagle motif in black and the name 'Toyo', no. 111 with a dragon in black and the name 'Zugi', and no. 115 with a four-leaf clover in green, this being the personal marking of *ppłk dypl. pil.* Robert Cierniak, at the time commanding the 1. *elt*.

Another interesting feature on the aircraft based in Lithuania was the eagle eye motif on the air intakes. The eyes could be seen on the forward protection screens when the aircraft was parked or taxiing. They survive on all four aircraft to date.

In 2008 a similar mission was undertaken by aircraft from the Malbork-based 41. *elt*. Four machines, nos. 4101, 4104, 4113, and 4120 took part in the *PKW-2 Orlik*. The emblem of the mission, similar to that of the first *PKW* but smaller, was applied immediately aft of the Polish national markings on the fins.

[23, 24]: 1. PLM/1. elt *emblems with 'plm' (for 'Pułk Lotnictwa Myśliwskiego', 'Fighter Aviation Regiment') on the wave motif under the 'Mermaid' badge, 2002.*
[25, 26]: 1. elt *emblems without the 'plm' on the wave, 2005.*
[27]: *The 'Kościuszko' badge (dating back to the 'Kościuszko' Squadron of US volunteers in the 1920 Polish-Russian war and also used by 303 Squadron during WWII) on '40', 2006.*
[28]: 41. elt *armament section badge, 2007. The 'Toruń Duck' was the traditional badge of pre-war Toruń-based fighter units and of 306 Squadron during WWII).*

Polish Wings

NO. 38 | MiG-29

MiG-29 no. 2960532038, '3810' of the 1st Squadron, 11th Fighter Regiment, Žatec, Czech Republic. Mińsk Mazowiecki 22 December 1995. Aircraft in original Czech camouflage and markings.

[30-32]: The aircraft upon delivery to Poland. Note the national markings of the Czech Republic, the 'tiger' motif on the fins and the emblem of the 1st Squadron, 11th Fighter Regiment at Žatec.
In Polish service the aircraft had Polish national markings and the 1. PLM emblem applied, but the 'tiger' motif was retained on the fins. The Czech code nos. on the fins and the Czech unit emblem were removed. Two-digit code numbers were applied on the sides of the engine air intakes. Mińsk Mazowiecki, December 1995.

NO. 38 | MiG-29   **Polskie Skrzydła**

[33] MiG-29 no. 2960532038, '38' of the 1. PLM; 'Eagle's Talon' Exercise, 1997. Aircraft in Czech scheme with Polish national markings.

[34]: The aircraft photographed at Powidz air base and 2001 in the new camouflage scheme applied during overhaul at WZL-2 in Bydgoszcz (1st period).
[35]: This machine was the first to have the black anti-glare panel, painted by WZL-2, forward of the cockpit. Radom Air Show 2003.
[36]: MiG-29 '38' photographed at Malbork air base. Note signs of wear on the fuselage. September 2004.

Polish Wings

NO. 38 | MiG-29

[37]: In 2004 the aircraft received the Kościuszko badge on the port side under the cockpit. About the same time the nose radome from another aircraft was fitted and a patch of new paint was applied on the port wing tip. Mińsk Mazowiecki, June 2004.
[38]: Starboard fin and rudder, June 2005.
[39]: The 'Mermaid' and Kościuszko badges. Mińsk Mazowiecki, June 2005.

[40]: Rear view of the same aircraft. Note the traces of wear on the vertical tail units, Mińsk Mazowiecki 2006.

[41]: A good view of the top surfaces. Note that the upper flaps of the air intakes are open, which indicates that the aircraft is performing an energetic manoeuvre, August 2006.

NO. 38 | MiG-29 **Polskie Skrzydła**

[42]: In 2007 a patch of new paint was applied on the starboard wing-fuselage joint. It was in this scheme with visible traces of wear that the aircraft was sent away for an overhaul in 2007. Mińsk Mazowiecki, September 2007.

[43]: Mińsk Mazowiecki, August 2007.

[44]: Mińsk Mazowiecki, October 2007.

17

Polish Wings

NO. 38 | MiG-29

[45, 46, 47]: An aircraft in the maintenance hangar. Note the traces of wear on the vertical tail and sides of the fuselage. Note the patch of new paint under the cockpit in the bottom photo. Mińsk Mazowiecki, August 2007.

[48]: '38' prepared for flight, patches of the new paint are visible.
[49]: Post-flight servicing of '38', Malbork, July 2007.
[50]: An aircraft towed to the apron, Mińsk Mazowiecki, August 2007.

NO. 38 | MiG-29 　　　　　　　　　　　　　　　　　　　　　　Polskie Skrzydła

48

49

50

19

Polish Wings NO. 38 | MiG-29

[51]

[51]: *Rear view of an aircraft taking off. '38' after the major overhaul (2nd period) completed in 2009. The machine was undergoing the overhaul for two years before it returned to the 1. elt. Aircraft in the new scheme.*

[52]: *Starboard view of '38' on the apron. Mińsk Mazowiecki, August 2009.*

[53]: *An aircraft towed out of the hardened shelter. Upper surfaces of the fuselage and wings are shown to advantage. Mińsk Mazowiecki August 2009.*

[52]

[53]

NO. 38 | MiG-29

Polskie Skrzydła

[54, 55]: Take-off and landing of an aircraft at Mińsk Mazowiecki, December 2009.

54

55

56 *MiG-29 no. 2960532038, '38' of the 1. elt; Mińsk Mazowiecki, December 2009. Aircraft in the new scheme received during major overhaul at WZL-2 (2nd period).*

21

Polish Wings

NO. 40 | MiG-29

57 MiG-29 no. 2960532040, '40' of the 1. PLM, Mińsk Mazowiecki, 1997.
Aircraft in Czech scheme with Polish national markings.

58 MiG-29 no. 2960532040, '40' of the 1. elt, Mińsk Mazowiecki, February 2002.
Aircraft in post major overhaul scheme (1st period).

22

[59-67] An aircraft in post-overhaul scheme (1st period). Note traces of wear after long operation and the PKW 'Orlik' badge applied in January 2006. The aircraft featured patches of a different colour on the wing tips applied during upgrade work at WZL-2 Bydgoszcz. Since 2004 the aircraft featured a nose radome from another machine. During late 2005 the machine received the Kościuszko badge on the port side under the cockpit.

[59]: Powidz, March 2003.
[60]: Radom, September 2003.
[61]: Mińsk Mazowiecki, March 2007.
[62]: Mińsk Mazowiecki, October 2008.
[63]: Mińsk Mazowiecki, October 2007.
[64]: Mińsk Mazowiecki, March 2007.
[65]: The badge of the PKW 'Orlik' – the Polish contingent of the Baltic Air Policing mission at Siauliai in Lithuania in 2006. The badge was applied on the outer surfaces of the fins of aircraft nos. '40', '77', '111' and '115'.
[66]: The 'eagle eyes' were applied on engine air intake covers during the PKW 'Orlik' mission to Lithuania.
[67]: A machine armed with B-8 pods with S-8 unguided rockets. Mińsk Mazowiecki, March 2007.

Polish Wings

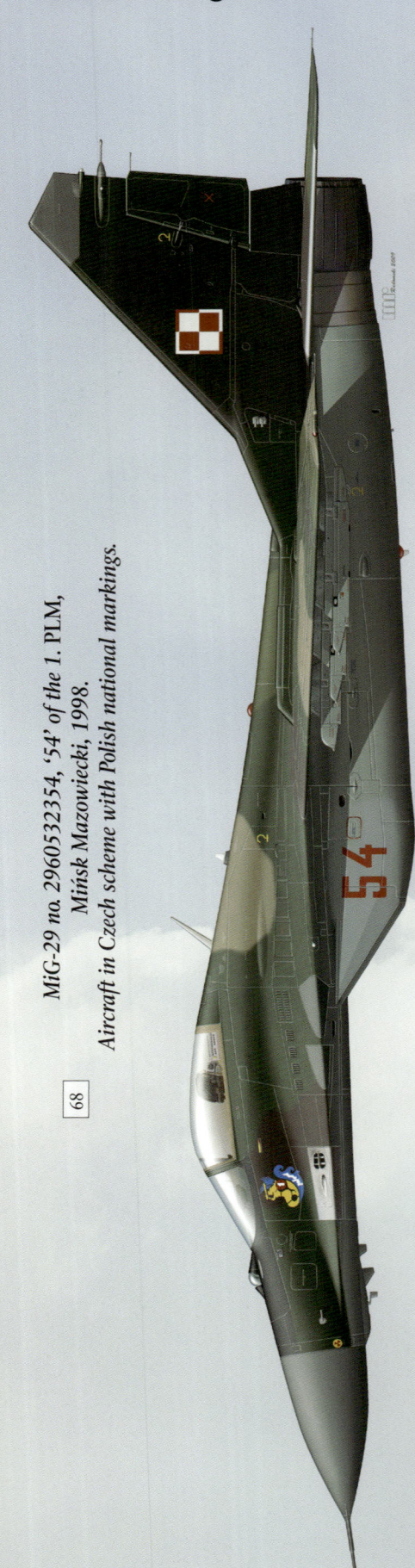

NO. 54 | MiG-29

[69-71]: An aircraft in the Czech camouflage scheme but with the Polish code no. 54 and Polish national markings. The machine does not have the 'tiger' motif on the fins. In January 1996 the badge of the 1. PLM was applied on both sides of the forward fuselage.

[69]: Bydgoszcz Air Show in 1996.
[70]: An aircraft taxiing after the display at Bydgoszcz in 1996.
[71]: '54' in flight, armed with the R-73 AAM.

[68] MiG-29 na 2960532354, '54' of the 1. PLM, Mińsk Mazowiecki, 1998. Aircraft in Czech scheme with Polish national markings.

24

[72-75]: *An aircraft in its new post-overhaul scheme (1st period). It features the 1. PLM badge without the letters 'plm' on the blue wave. June 2006 [72]. Mińsk Mazowiecki, October 2004 [73], August 2008 [74, 75].*

Polish Wings

NO. 54 | MiG-29

MiG-29 no. 2960532354, '54' of the 1. elt, Mińsk Mazowiecki, 2004. Aircraft with post overhaul scheme (1st period) with patches of new paint.

NO. 54 | MiG-29 — Polskie Skrzydła

[77-81]: In November 2008 the aircraft received patches of new paint in the badly worn light grey areas, and the 'Mermaid' badge on both sides of the fuselage was refreshed. Mińsk Mazowiecki, November 2008.

Polish Wings NO. 56 | MiG-29

MiG-29 no. 2960532356, '56' of the 1. PLM, Mińsk Mazowiecki, 1996. Aircraft in Czech scheme with Polish national isignia.

NO. 56 | MiG-29

Polskie Skrzydła

[84]: *An aircraft after a retouched paint job in 2004. Note clear traces of wear following long operation. The aircraft is fitted with a UR-60 short range practice AAM. October 2004.*

[85]: *In 2005 aircraft received the Kościuszko badge on the port side under the cockpit. Mińsk Mazowiecki, June 2006.*

[86]: *'56' in flight at high altitude, April 2005.*

MiG-29 no. 2960532356, '56' of the 1. elt, Mińsk Mazowiecki, 2001. Aircraft in post-overhaul (1st period scheme.

29

Polish Wings | NO. 56 | MiG-29

[87]: An aircraft following more retouching in 2007. In March 2007 the red 'Dragon-Griffon' badge was applied at the base of the port fin. '56' ready for towing, April 2007, Mińsk Mazowiecki.

[88 – 90]: Mińsk Mazowiecki 2007.

[91]: The unofficial badge of the 1. elt's section III from March 2007. In absence of a better photo this is an enlarged fragment of a bigger image. The badge was designed and applied by mł. chor *Paweł Giec*.

NO. 56 | MiG-29   **Polskie Skrzydła**

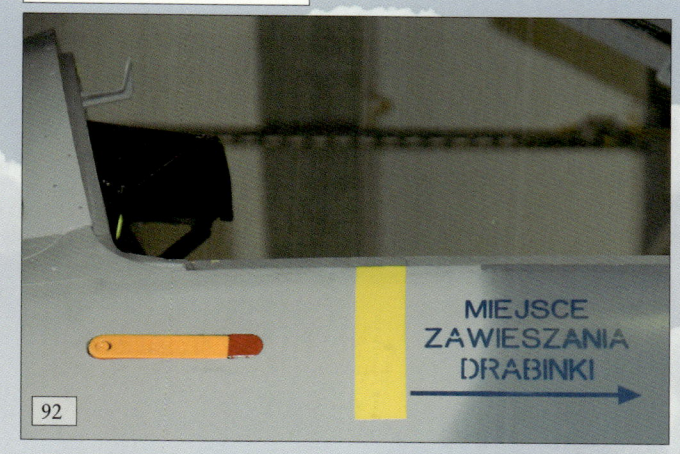

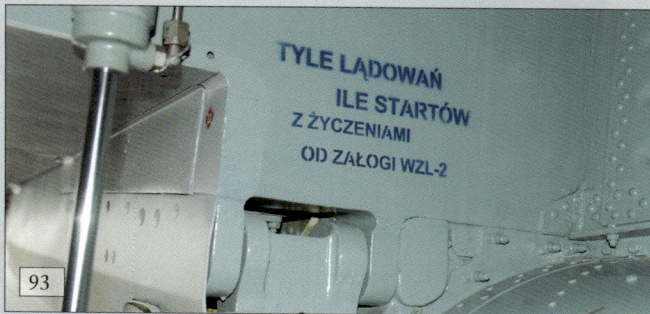

[92, 93]: Following an overhaul (2nd period) the aircraft received new scheme and previously unseen stencils: 'Ladder attachment location' and 'As many landings as take-offs with best wishes from WZL-2 crew', 2009.
[94]: Top surface of the tailplane and the fins and rudders in the post-overhaul scheme, Mińsk Mazowiecki November 2009.
[95]: Flight-ready '56' in the hardened shelter at Mińsk Mazowiecki, December 2009.

31

Polish Wings

NO. 59 | MiG-29

[96] MiG-29 no. 2960532359, '5918' of 1st Squadron, 11th Fighter Regiment, Žatec, Czech Republic. Mińsk Mazowiecki 22 December 1995. Aircraft in the original Czech scheme.

[96]: An aircraft in the Czech camouflage. Note the 'tiger' motif on the fin. The machine has Polish markings and the new code no. 59 applied on the air intakes. It was used in this scheme by the 1. PLM for four years.

[97] MiG-29 no. 2960532359, '59' of the 1. PLM, Mińsk Mazowiecki, 1997. Aircraft in Czech scheme with Polish national markings.

32

NO. 59 | MiG-29   **Polskie Skrzydła**

98

MiG-29 no. 296052359, '59' of the 1. PLM, Mińsk Mazowiecki, 2000.
Aircraft in post-overhaul scheme (1st period).

99

MiG-29 no. 296052359, '59' of the 1. PLM, Mińsk Mazowiecki, 2005.
Aircraft in post-overhaul scheme (1st period) with retouches of new paint.

[99]: *Following an accident this aircraft had the port vertical tail replaced and the starboard one repaired. Both inner and outer camouflage patterns on the vertical tails were changed. Other components of the aircraft and their painting scheme were unchanged.*

33

Polish Wings

NO. 59 | MiG-29

[100]

[100-102]: *An aircraft in its post-repair scheme. In 2005 this machine received the Kościuszko badge on the port side under the cockpit. In 2008 it was sent away for a major overhaul while still in the same scheme.*

[100]: *'59' in flight at high altitude, armed with R-73 short range AAMs, 2004.*

[101]: *'59' during an inspection in the maintenance hangar at Malbork, 2006.*

[102]: *'59' taking off for a sortie to the naval firing range off Ustka. The R-73 missile carried on the under-wing launcher is going to be fired against a CP-100 airborne target.*

[101]

[102]

NO. 65 | MiG-29　　　　　　　　　　　　　　　　　　　　　　　　　　**Polskie Skrzydła**

MiG-29 no. 2960526365, '65' of the 1. PLM, Mińsk Mazowiecki, 1995. Aircraft in Russian delivery scheme. In 1994 the aircraft received its first patches of new paint: on wing leading edges and on the vertical tail.

[104-106]: The aircraft with special emblems to celebrate 65 years of 'Skrzydlata Polska' aviation magazine. Silhouettes of the pre-WWII RWD light sports aeroplane and the MiG-29 were applied on the air intakes. These were then overpainted during the same year. The aircraft was then used in this scheme until a major overhaul in 1998. Mińsk Mazowiecki 1995.

Polish Wings

NO. 65 | MiG-29

MiG-29 in the post-overhaul scheme (1st period). The 'Mermaid' badge was applied on both sides of the forward fuselage. The unchanged scheme, with clear signs of extensive use, was retained until another major overhaul in 2008.
[107]: Powidz, March 2003.
[108]: Mińsk Mazowiecki, December 2005,
[109]: '65' taking off with another MiG from Mińsk Mazowiecki, June 2006. Note signs of extensive wear.

[110] MiG-29 no. 296052 6365, '65' of the 1. elt, Mińsk Mazowiecki, 2004. Aircraft in the post-overhaul scheme (1st period).

36

NO. 65 | MiG-29

Polskie Skrzydła

[111, 112]: '65' following the major overhaul by WZL-2 in Bydgoszcz in 2008 (2nd period). Aircraft in the new scheme. Several days after delivery to the 41. elt the aircraft received the unit badge (on both sides of the cockpit), and then the emblem of the maintenance section was applied on the starboard air intake. Emblems see page 13.

Polish Wings

NO. 66 | MiG-29

[113]: '66' in the factory (Russian delivery) scheme. From the very beginning the machine featured the 1. PLM badge and dark background to the code numbers on both sides of the air intakes. Powidz 1991.

[114]: An aircraft following a major overhaul at WZL-2 Bydgoszcz, (1st period), aircraft in the new scheme. The machine received the badge of the 1. PLM. Mińsk Mazowiecki, March 2003.

[115]: In 2004 this aircraft received the nose radome from another machine. '66' continued to be used in this scheme until 2006 when it was sent away for an overhaul. Malbork, August 2004.

[116, 117]: '66' during servicing at Malbork air base. Note the light grey nose radome, probably coming from another aircraft. Malbork 2003.

38

NO. 66 | MiG-29   Polskie Skrzydła

MiG-29 na 296526366, '66' of the 1. elt, Mińsk Mazowiecki, 2004. Aircraft in the post-overhaul scheme (1st period)

[118]

[119]

[120]

[119-121]: An aircraft after its second major overhaul at WZL-2 Bydgoszcz, (2nd period). Aircraft in the new scheme. This machine was delivered to the 41. elt at Malbork and it features the unit badge on both sides of the forward fuselage.

[119]: Aircraft ready for a training sortie. Malbork, December 2009.
[120]: '66', armed with the R-60 short range AAMs at QRA readiness at Mińsk Mazowiecki, September 2008.
[121]: '66' taxiing after a sortie to Jagodne training range during exercises of the 1. Skrzydło Lotnictwa Taktycznego (1st Tactical Wing). Mińsk Mazowiecki, October 2008.

[121]

39

Polish Wings | NO. 66 | MiG-29

MiG-29 no. 2960526366, '66' of the 41. elt, Malbork, 2008. Aircraft in the post-overhaul scheme (2nd period).

NO. 67 | MiG-29   **Polskie Skrzydła**

[123 – 125]: '67' in the factory applied camouflage (Russian delivery) scheme. The pattern was different from all other MiG-29 aircraft delivered to Poland. Poznań-Krzesiny 1991.

[126]: An aircraft after some retouching of the paint scheme. Grey paint was applied on both air intakes, wing leading edges and at the wing-fuselage joint near the cockpit. Bydgoszcz 1997.

Polish Wings

NO. 67 | MiG-29

127 — MiG-29 no. 296052636/ '67' of the 1. PLM, Mińsk Mazowiecki, 1997. An aircraft in Russian delivery scheme with additional grey paint areas on both air intakes, wing edges and at the wing-fuselage joint near the cockpit. The 'Mermaid' badge was applied on both sides of the fuselage.

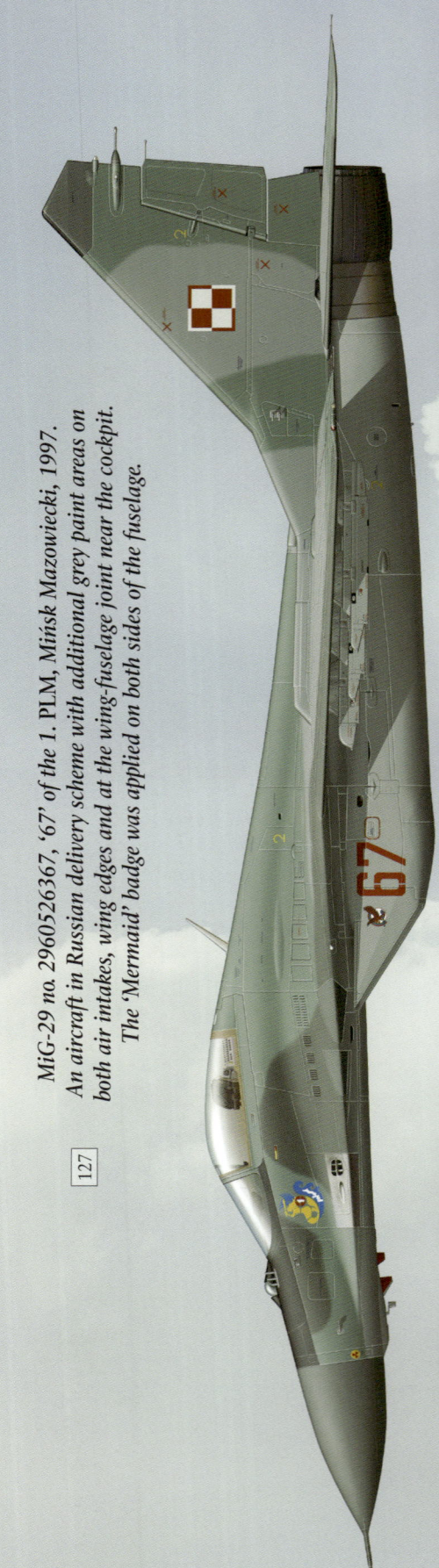

[128, 129]: '67' in the new camouflage scheme following a major overhaul at WZL-2, (1st period). Note the absence of the 'Mermaid' badge. The Kościuszko badge was applied on the port side of the fuselage in 2004.

[130]: '67' received the Kościuszko badge in 2004. The aircraft continued to be used in this colour scheme until October 2008.

NO. 67 | MiG-29

Polskie Skrzydła

MiG-29 no. 296526367, '67' of the 1. elt, Mińsk Mazowiecki, 2004. Aircraft in post-overhaul scheme, (1st period)

131

43

Polish Wings

NO. 67 | MiG-29

[132-136]: An aircraft following camouflage retouching in October 2008. The paint coat was refreshed before the planned departure to Scotland for an international exercise (that eventually did not materialise due to adverse weather). New paint can be seen under the cockpit, on wing edges and air intakes.

NO. 67 | MiG-29

Polskie Skrzydła

[137]: '67' towed to the engine test stand, January 2009.
[138]: MiG-29 ready for a training sortie, Mińsk Mazowiecki, December 2008.

NO. 70 | MiG-29

[139]: '70' in the factory applied camouflage scheme (Russian delivery). The 'Mermaid' badge of the 1. PLM was applied on both sides of the fuselage. Powidz, June 1991.

Polish Wings | NO. 70 | MiG-29

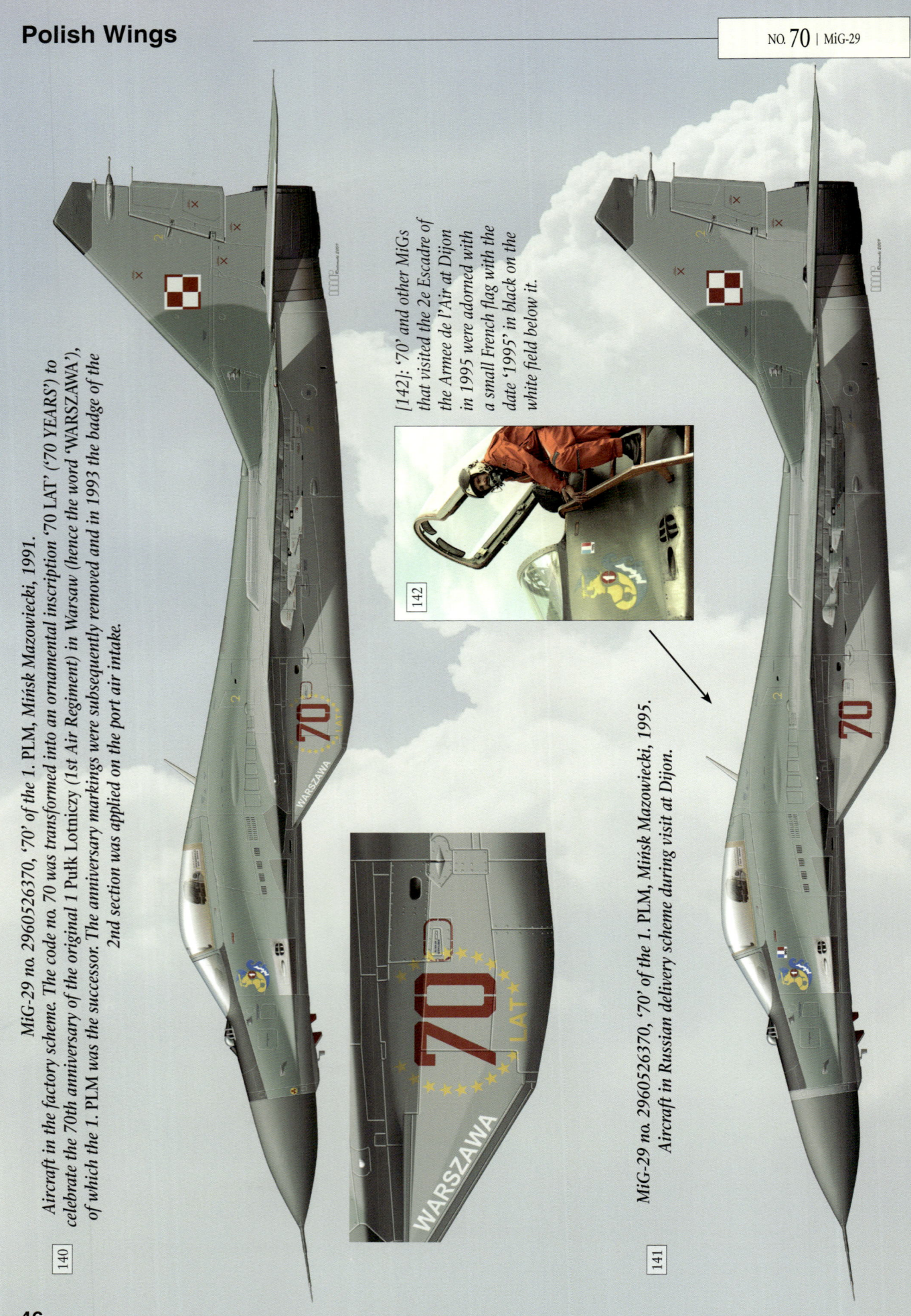

[140] MiG-29 no. 2960526370, '70' of the 1. PLM, Mińsk Mazowiecki, 1991. Aircraft in the factory scheme. The code no. 70 was transformed into an ornamental inscription '70 LAT' ('70 YEARS') to celebrate the 70th anniversary of the original 1 Pułk Lotniczy (1st Air Regiment) in Warsaw (hence the word 'WARSZAWA'), of which the 1. PLM was the successor. The anniversary markings were subsequently removed and in 1993 the badge of the 2nd section was applied on the port air intake.

[142]: '70' and other MiGs that visited the 2e Escadre of the Armee de l'Air at Dijon in 1995 were adorned with a small French flag with the date '1995' in black on the white field below it.

[141] MiG-29 no. 2960526370, '70' of the 1. PLM, Mińsk Mazowiecki, 1995. Aircraft in Russian delivery scheme during visit at Dijon.

46

NO. 70 | MiG-29   Polskie Skrzydła

[143]: Mińsk Mazowiecki, August 1995. An aircraft in the factory camouflage with numerous patches of refreshed colours. New paint was applied on the entire nose, on the wing leading edges and at the base of the fins. This aircraft was used in this paint scheme until it was earmarked for major overhaul in 1997.

[144]: DOL (Drogowy Odcinek Lotniskowy, *Highway Airstrip*) Kliniska, June 1995.
[145]: Mińsk Mazowiecki, October 1995.

Polish Wings

NO. 70 | MiG-29

[146]: An aircraft photographed in 2000 in its new scheme after the first major overhaul by WZL-2 Bydgoszcz (1st period). This was the first MiG-29 to undergo a major overhaul in Poland and it received the newly designed three-tone camouflage. The aircraft was adorned with the 'Mermaid' badge on both sides of the fuselage.

[147]: MiG-29 '70' with the name of the 1. PLM commander applied temporarily during the exercise at DOL Kliniska in 2000.

[148, 149]: An aircraft with new paint patches on the port side of the forward fuselage. Radom 2001.

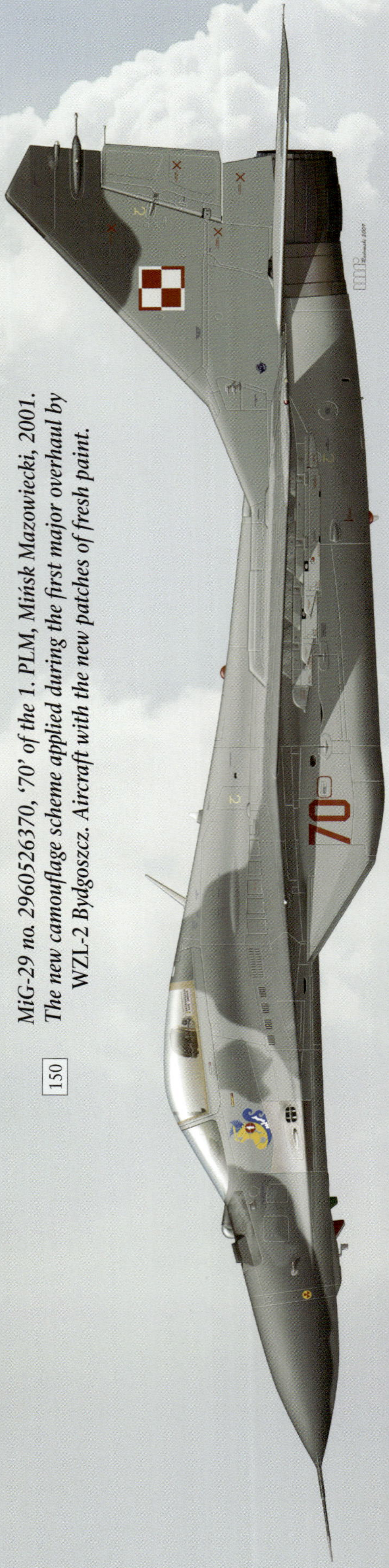

[150]: MiG-29 no. 296052637O, '70' of the 1. PLM, Mińsk Mazowiecki, 2001. The new camouflage scheme applied during the first major overhaul by WZL-2 Bydgoszcz. Aircraft with the new patches of fresh paint.

48

NO. 70 | MiG-29   **Polskie Skrzydła**

[151, 152]: An aircraft in its latest scheme after the second overhaul by WZL-2 Bydgoszcz (2nd period). The aircraft was delivered to the 41. elt at Malbork. It received the 41. elt badge on both sides of the fuselage. Malbork, June 2007.
[153, 154]: Malbork, September 2008.
[155]: Mińsk Mazowiecki, October 2008. '70' on the left with '4103' right.

Polish Wings

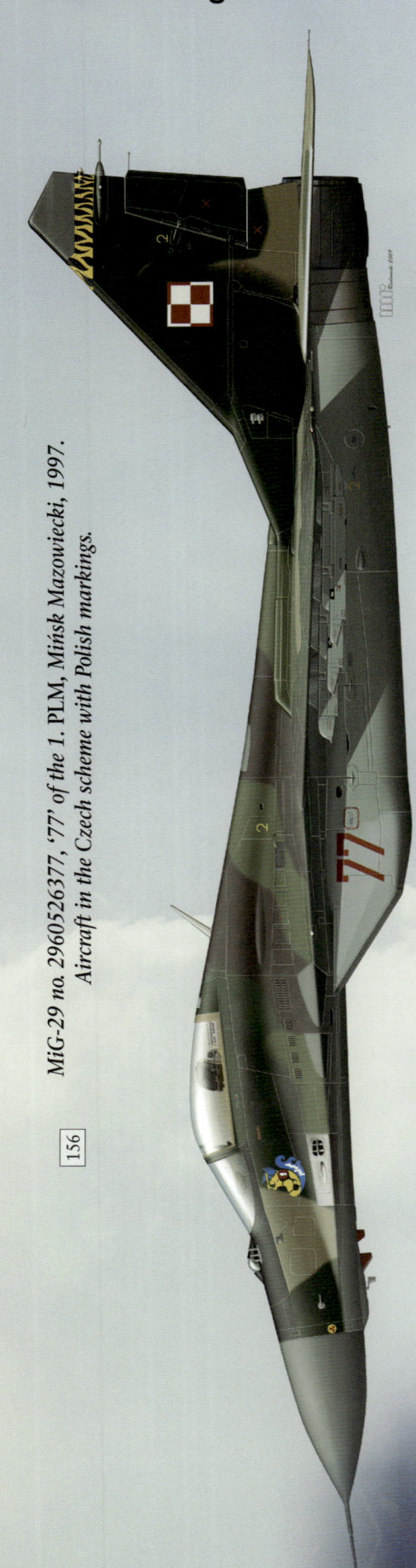

NO. 77 | MiG-29

[157]: Aircraft in Czech camouflage with Polish national markings and the '77' code no. on the air intakes. This machine retained the 'tiger' motif at the top of the fins. The 1. PLM badge was applied on both sides of the forward fuselage in January 1996. May 1997.

[158]: Aircraft in the new scheme, applied in 1999, after the first overhaul by WZL-2 Bydgoszcz (1st period). The Kościuszko badge was applied on the port side under the cockpit during 2004. Łask, 2004.

[159]: MiG-29 and Mirage 2000, 2003.

MiG-29 no. 296052637, '77' of the 1. PLM, Mińsk Mazowiecki, 1997. Aircraft in the Czech scheme with Polish markings.

50

NO. 77 | MiG-29   **Polskie Skrzydła**

[160]: Mińsk Mazowiecki, June 2006.
[161]: In January 2006 '77' received the 'PKW "Orlik"' badge on the fins and a personal emblem (attacking bird and the name 'TOYO') aft of the cockpit. Additionally, the machine's finish was retouched on all upper surfaces. The pale patches on wing tips were applied during upgrade work at WZL-2 Bydgoszcz. The machine wore this camouflage scheme when it was sent for another overhaul at WZL-2 Bydgoszcz. Mińsk Mazowiecki, September 2006.
[162]: Mińsk Mazowiecki, October 2006.

Polish Wings NO. 77 | MiG-29

[163]: '77' following a major overhaul by WZL-2 Bydgoszcz in 2009 (2nd period). The machine was delivered from the 1. elt to the 41. elt to make up numbers. It displays the 41. elt badge on both sides of the fuselage under the cockpit. The 'Toruń duck' emblem of the 41. elt maintenance section was applied on the port air intake. Aircraft in the new scheme.

[164]: The 41. PLM badge, which included a plan view of the MiG-21 wing and tail, was retained by the 41. elt and is applied on its MiG-29s.

[165]: '77' armed with the R-73 medium range AAMs at QRA readiness at Malbork air base, September 2009.

Polskie Skrzydła

166 MiG-29 no. 296526377, '77' of the 41. elt, Malbork, 2009. Aircraft in the post-overhaul scheme (2nd period).

167 [167]: MiG-29 '77' photographed in June 2009 at Malbork air base.

Polish Wings

NO. 83 | MiG-29

[168] MiG-29 no 296026383 '83' of the 1. PLM, Mińsk Mazowiecki, 1996. Aircraft in Czech scheme with Polish national markings.

[169]: Wielkopolska region, September 1997. The white band was applied on the rear fuselage and fins for the exercise 'Eagle's Talon 97'.

[170]: Powidz air base 14 September 1997, exercise 'Eagle's Talon 97'.

[171]: Bydgoszcz 2002. This aircraft sported Czech camouflage with Polish national markings and the code number '83' on the air intakes. The 'tiger' motifs at the top of the fins were retained and the 'Mermaid' badge of the 1. PLM was applied under the cockpit. When delivered for major overhaul in 2002 it no longer had the white band, and the national markings were in the modified style (with the colours reversed).

NO. 83 | MiG-29   **Polskie Skrzydła**

[172]: Poznań-Krzesiny, September 2003. '83' in the new scheme after its first overhaul (1st period). Initially no 'Mermaid' badge was carried on either side of the fuselage.

[173, 174]: The same aircraft with a patch of new paint on the port side of the forward fuselage near the cockpit. The aircraft received the 'Mermaid' badge on both sides of the forward fuselage and the Kościuszko badge on the port side under the cockpit. August 2006 [173], September 2007 [174].

Polish Wings

NO. 83 | MiG-29

[175-179]: MiG-29 '83' at Mińsk Mazowiecki. The aircraft has the 'Mermaid' and Kościuszko badges. Patches of fresh paint on the wing tips and on the port side under the cockpit are visible.
The photos depict the aircraft: in 2005 [175], 2006 [176, 177], 2007 [178], August 2008 [179].

NO. 83 | MiG-29

Polskie Skrzydła

[180] Aircraft after some repainting of the inboard surface of the port fin. Mińsk Mazowiecki 8 August 2007, parked right to left: '83', '54', '111'. October 2007. [181], September 2008. [182], October 2008 [183]. In 2009 the machine was sent away for an overhaul at WZL-2 Bydgoszcz.

57

Polish Wings

NO. 89 | MiG-29

[185]: Poznań-Krzesiny, May 1996. Aircraft in Czech camouflage, with Polish national markings and the code number 89. The machine features the 'tiger' motif at the fin tips. The badge of the 1. PLM was applied in January 1996 on both sides of the forward fuselage.

[186]: Poznań-Krzesiny, September 1997. In 1997 a white band was applied on the rear fuselage for the 'Eagle's Talon '97' exercise.

[187]: Mińsk Mazowiecki 1998, with white band removed.

Mikoyan MiG-29 296052 6389, '89' of the 1. PLM, Mińsk Mazowiecki, 1997. Aircraft in the Czech scheme with Polish national markings.

58

Polskie Skrzydła

MiG-29 no. 2960526389, '89' of the 1. elt, Mińsk Mazowiecki, 2004. Aircraft in the post-overhaul scheme, (1st period)

Polish Wings

NO. 89 | MiG-29

[189]: '89' in flight at high altitude in the camouflage scheme it received after the first major overhaul at WZL-2 Bydgoszcz, 2004.
[190]: Mińsk Mazowiecki, October 2005.
[191]: Łask, September 2004.
[192]: Aircraft with patches of new paint on the port side of the nose radome-fuselage joint. In 2005 it received the Kościuszko badge on the port side under the cockpit. March 2008.
[193]: MiG-29 '89'. Note patches of new paint on the starboard side of the forward fuselage. The aircraft shows signs of extensive wear. September 2008. In this form it went to WZL-2 Bydgoszcz for another overhaul.

NO. 92 | MiG-29

Polskie Skrzydła

[194] MiG-29 no. 2960526392, '92' of the 1. PLM, Mińsk Mazowiecki, 1997. Aircraft in the Czech Scheme with Polish national markings. In 1997 a white band was applied on the rear fuselage for the 'Eagle's Talon '97' exercise.

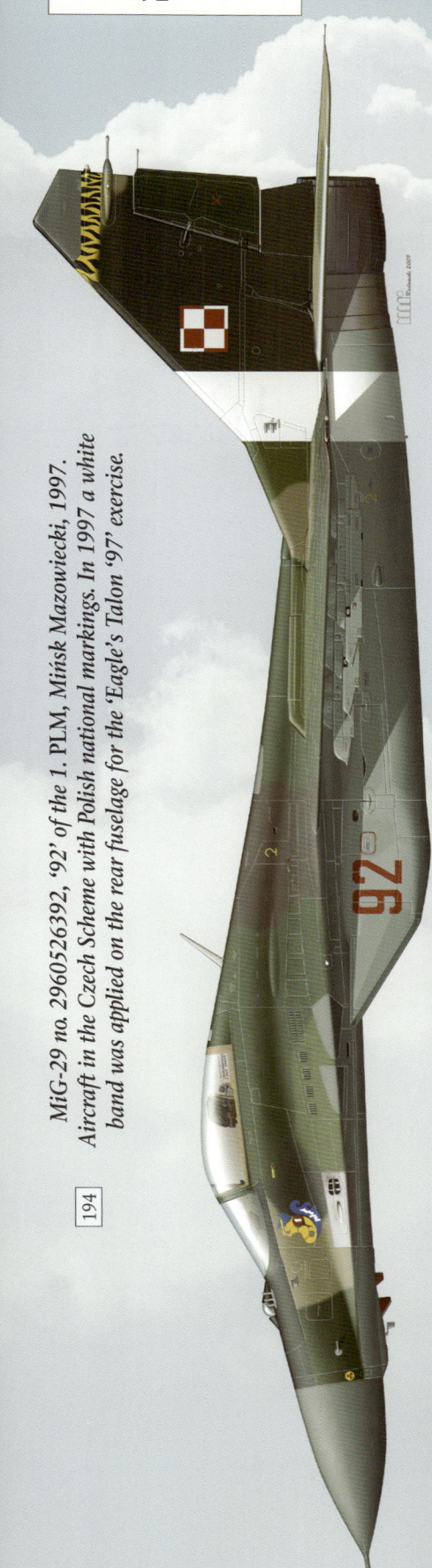

[195]: Mińsk Mazowiecki, October 1997. '92' in Czech camouflage. The machine features the 'tiger' motif at the fin tips. In January 1996 the Czech roundels, code numbers on the fins and the badge of the 1. Stíhací Letecký Pluk (1st Air Regiment) CzAF from Žatec were replaced with Polish national markings, Polish codes on air intakes and the 'Mermaid' badge on the forward fuselage.

[196]: Mińsk Mazowiecki 1999. After the first overhaul at WZL-2 Bydgoszcz. Aircraft in the new scheme. The regimental 'Mermaid' badge was applied on both sides of the forward fuselage upon arrival at the 1. PLM.

[197]: Powidz, September 2004.

61

Polish Wings

NO. 92 | MiG-29

198 MiG-29 no. 296526392, '92' of the 1. PLM, 'RIAT 2000', Cottesmore, UK, July 2000. Aircraft in the post-overhaul scheme (1st period).

[199-201]: After the second overhaul at WZL-2 (2nd period) this aircraft was delivered to the 41. elt at Malbork. The machine features the 41. elt badge on both sides of the fuselage.

62

NO. 92 | MiG-29

Polskie Skrzydła

202 MiG-29 no. 2960526392, '92' of the 41. elt, Malbork, 2008. Aircraft in the post-overhaul scheme (2nd period).

63

Polish Wings

NO. 92 | MiG-29

203

204

206

[203-204]: Aircraft No. 92 in flight to Nadarzyce firing ground on 15 September 2009. Aircraft was armed with two B-8 containers with S-8 unguided rockets.
[205]: This aircraft carries unguided rocket launchers under the wings.
[206]: Badge of 41. elt.

205

64

NO. 105 | MiG-29   **Polskie Skrzydła**

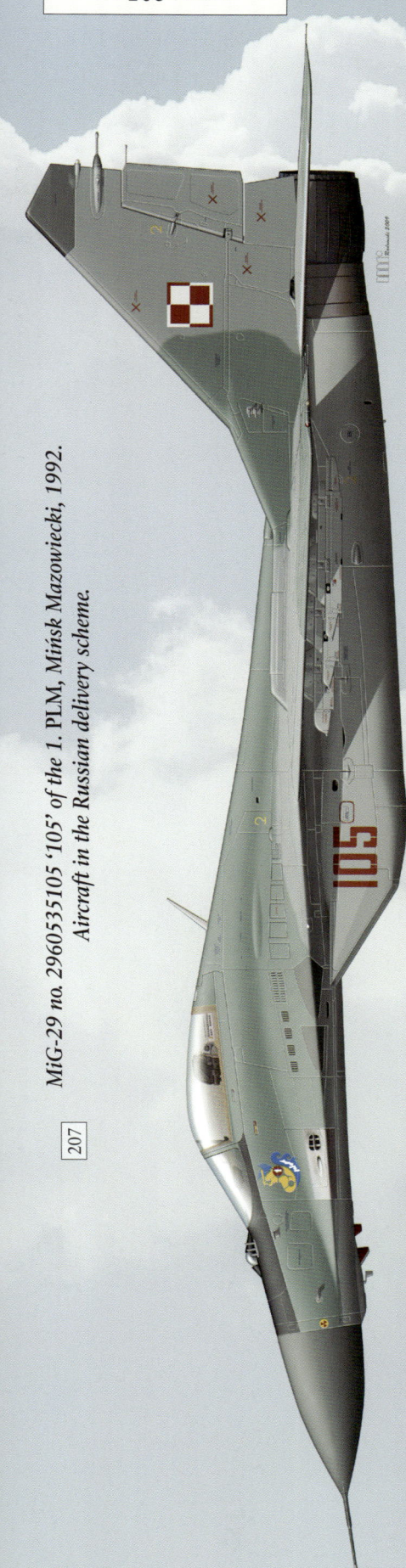

[208]: Dęblin, August 1995. '105' in the factory applied camouflage scheme. It features the 'Mermaid' badge of the 1. PLM on both sides of the fuselage. In 1993 the machine received the badge of the 2nd section forward of the code number on the port side.

[209]: '105' at Mierzęcice air base, readied for departure to an air show in Belgium, 1996. It sports the badge of the French 2^e Escadre under the cockpit (see profile 211).

[210]: Poznań-Krzesiny, June 1997. Aircraft with patches of new paint on the air intakes. In 1997 it took part in flight testing in Israel, and for the duration of those the Polish national markings and the unit badge were obliterated and the badge of the Israeli test centre was applied on the fin. The latter was overpainted after the testing was completed. Upon return to Poland the 'Mermaid' of the 1. PLM was applied again on both sides of the fuselage. In this scheme the aircraft went to WZL-2 Bydgoszcz for a major overhaul (see profile 212).

MiG-29 no. 2960535105 '105' of the 1. PLM, Mińsk Mazowiecki, 1992. Aircraft in the Russian delivery scheme.

[207]

65

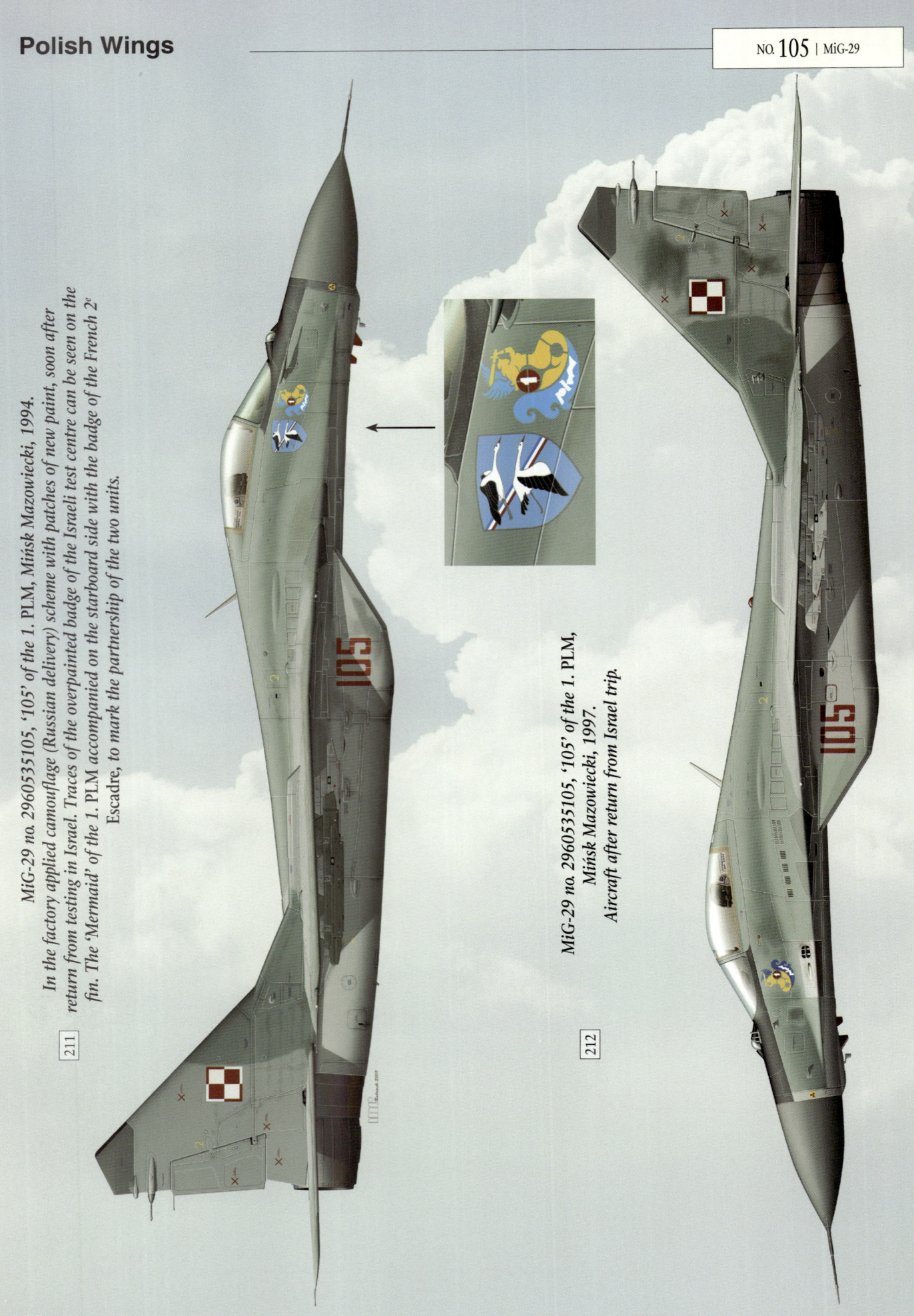

Polish Wings

NO. 105 | MiG-29

211 MiG-29 no. 2960535105, '105' of the 1. PLM, Mińsk Mazowiecki, 1994.
In the factory applied camouflage (Russian delivery) scheme with patches of new paint, soon after return from testing in Israel. Traces of the overpainted badge of the Israeli test centre can be seen on the fin. The 'Mermaid' of the 1. PLM accompanied on the starboard side with the badge of the French 2^e Escadre, to mark the partnership of the two units.

212 MiG-29 no. 2960535105, '105' of the 1. PLM, Mińsk Mazowiecki, 1997. Aircraft after return from Israel trip.

66

NO. 105 | MiG-29 　　　　　　　　　　　　　　　　　　　　　　　　**Polskie Skrzydła**

[213]: '105' in the new scheme after its first major overhaul at WZL-2 Bydgoszcz, (1st period), October 2005.
[214]: In 2006 the machine received the Kościuszko badge on the port side under the cockpit, September 2007.
[215]: Mińsk Mazowiecki, October 2008. By then the 'Mermaid' badge was applied on the starboard side of the fuselage (facing backwards).

67

Polish Wings

NO. 105 | MiG-29

MiG-29 no. 296053S105, '105' of the 1. elt, Mińsk Mazowiecki, 2008. Aircraft in the post-overhaul scheme (1st period).

[216]: Mińsk Mazowiecki, August 2008.
[217]: Mińsk Mazowiecki, October 2008.
[218]: The Kościuszko badge on the port side of the fuselage was obliterated. Mińsk Mazowiecki, September 2008.

68

NO. 105 | MiG-29

Polskie Skrzydła

220

221

[220 – 222]: '105' during climbing manoeuvres and towed on the airfield at Mińsk Mazowiecki. The machine still has the 'Mermaid' on the starboard side facing backwards. 2009.

222

Polish Wings NO. 105 | MiG-29

[223, 224]: '105' during an engine test and moments after take-off. Standard 'Mermaid' badge (facing forward) was applied on the port side fuselage, and the Kościuszko badge was re-applied under the cockpit. Mińsk Mazowiecki 2009.

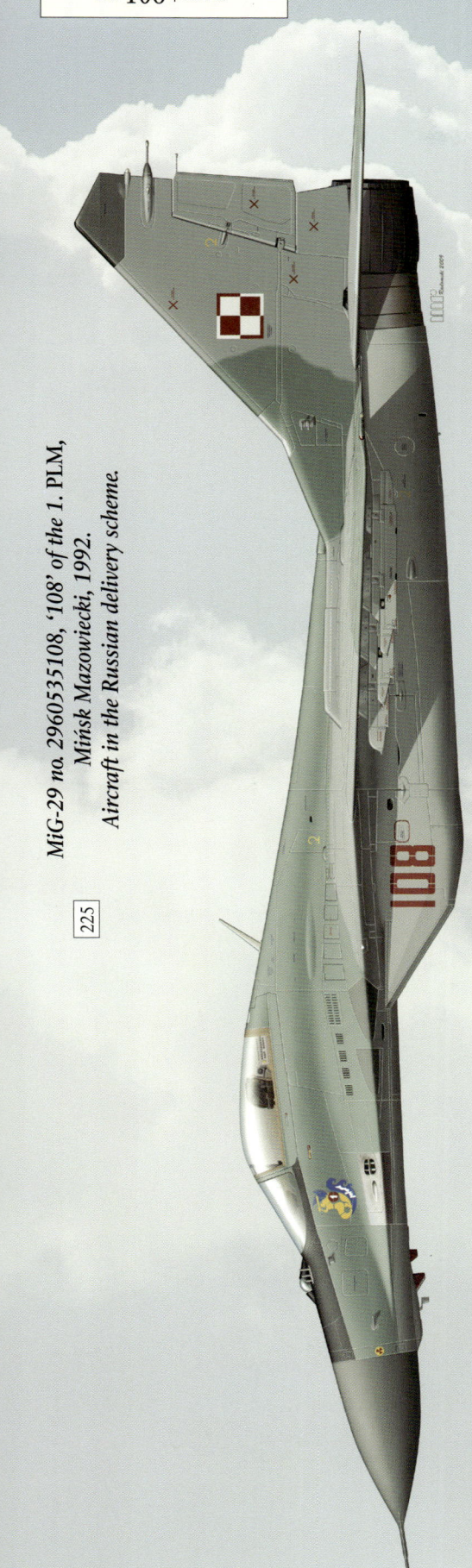

NO. 108 | MiG-29   Polskie Skrzydła

[225] MiG-29 no. 296053108, '108' of the 1. PLM, Mińsk Mazowiecki, 1992. Aircraft in the Russian delivery scheme.

[226]: '108' in the factory applied camouflage scheme. The machine features the 'Mermaid' badge of the 1. PLM on both sides of the fuselage. In 1993 the badge of the 2nd section was applied on the port air intake. Powidz 1991.

[227]: Mińsk Mazowiecki, June 1998. Note patches of new paint on wing leading edges, upper fuselage, fin edges and wing-fuselage joints. The machine has a grey band around the nose radome-fuselage joint.

[228, 229]: The badge of the 1st flight's 2nd section forward of the code number on the port air intake.

71

Polish Wings | NO. 108 | MiG-29

MiG-29 no. 2960535108, '108' of the 1. PLM, Mińsk Mazowiecki, 2000. Aircraft in the Russian delivery scheme.

[230]

[231]

[232]

[231]: Note patches of new paint on wing leading edges, upper fuselage, fin edges and wing-fuselage joints. The machine has a grey band around the nose radome-fuselage joint. The 'Mermaid' of the 1. PLM on both sides of the fuselage, and the 2nd section's badge forward of the code number on the port side. This aircraft retained this scheme, less the badge of the 2nd section, until major overhaul at WZL-2 Bydgoszcz. Mińsk Mazowiecki, February 1997.
[232]: Poznań-Krzesiny, June 1997.
[233]: DOL Kliniska 1999.

[233]

72

NO. 108 | MiG-29   **Polskie Skrzydła**

[234]: The new scheme after the first major overhaul at WZL-2 Bydgoszcz (1st period). The Kościuszko badge was applied on the port side of the fuselage under the cockpit. Mińsk Mazowiecki, August 2008.

[235]: Mińsk Mazowiecki, March 2007.
[236]: Mińsk Mazowiecki, June 2007.
[237]: Mińsk Mazowiecki, August 2008.

73

Polish Wings

NO. 108 | MiG-29

[238, 239]: '108' during preparations for night flying training. Note the 'Mermaid' badge without the usual red shield with 1 in white. Mińsk Mazowiecki, September 2009.

[240]: '108' about to take-off. A UR-60 practice missile can be seen under the wing. Note the 'Mermaid' badge without the red shield with 1 in white.

NO. 108 | MiG-29　　　　　　　　　　　　　　　　　　　　　　　　　　　**Polskie Skrzydła**

241

[241, 242]: '108' in flight. The 'Mermaid' is now complete with the shield and number 1. The photos were taken from MiG-29UB '28' near Wyszków, a town north-east of Warsaw, during air combat practice sortie. December 2009.

242

75

Polish Wings

NO. 111 | MiG-29

[244]: '111' in flight near Mińsk Mazowiecki. September 1997. Note the white band around the nose radome-fuselage joint and numerous patches of new paint.

[245]: Note new paint patches on wing leading edges, upper fuselage (from the cockpit up to the section between the engines), fin bases and wing-fuselage joints. The aircraft has the 'Mermaid' badge of the 1. PLM on both sides of the fuselage. In 1993 it received the badge of the 2nd section near the code number on the port side.

MiG-29 no. 2960535111, '111' of the 1. PLM, Mińsk Mazowiecki, 1993. Aircraft in the Russian delivery scheme.

76

NO. 111 | MiG-29

Polskie Skrzydła

MiG-29 no. 2960535111, '111' of the 1. PLM, Mińsk Mazowiecki, 1998. Aircraft in the Russian delivery scheme with new paint patches.

[247]: Aircraft with new paint patches on wing edges, upper fuselage, fin bases and wing-fuselage joints, and with a light grey nose radome from another aircraft. The aircraft has the 'Mermaid' badge of the 1. PLM on both sides of the fuselage. Mińsk Mazowiecki, March 1998. In this scheme, less the 2nd section badge, it went for a major overhaul to WZL-2 Bydgoszcz.
[248]: Mińsk Mazowiecki, May 2000.
[249]: Powidz 2000.

77

Polish Wings

NO. 111 | MiG-29

[250]: Dęblin, August 2003. '111' in the new scheme after the first major overhaul at WZL-2 Bydgoszcz (1st period). Note the absence of the 'Mermaid' badge.
[251]: Mińsk Mazowiecki, June 2006.

[252]: Mińsk Mazowiecki 2006. The aircraft already has the PKW 'Orlik' emblem on the fin.

NO. 111 | MiG-29 **Polskie Skrzydła**

[253, 254]: Aircraft in the post-overhaul scheme with the emblem of the PKW 'Orlik' Baltic Air Policing mission deployed to Lithuania in January 2006. The emblem was applied on both fins. A personal emblem in the form of a dragon motif with the name 'ZUGI' was applied on both sides of the fuselage aft of the cockpit. 'Eyes' were painted on the air intake covers.

[255, 256]: '111' in the post-overhaul scheme with the PKW 'Orlik' emblems and the Kościuszko badge on the port side of the fuselage.

Polish Wings

NO. 111 | MiG-29

257 MiG-29 nr. 2960535111, '111' of por. pil. Grzegorz 'Zugi' Zugaj, 1. elt, Mińsk Mazowiecki, 2006. Aircraft in the post-overhaul scheme (1st period) with additional markings.

258 [258]: '111' taking off with full afterburner, Mińsk Mazowiecki, October 2008.

80

NO. 114 | MiG-29

Polskie Skrzydła

[259]: '114' in Russian delivery scheme with fresh paint areas after the Israeli trip. It received the white quick recognition band on the rear fuselage for the exercise 'Eagle's Talon '97'. Poznań-Krzesiny, September 1997.
[260]: September 1997.
[261]: October 1998.

81

Polish Wings

NO. 114 | MiG-29

MiG-29 no. 2960535114, '114' of płk. pil. Stefan Rutkowski, commanding the 1. elt, Mińsk Mazowiecki, 2007. Aircraft in the post-overhaul scheme (1st period).

262

82

NO. 114 | MiG-29　　　　　　　　　　　　　　　　　　　　　　　　**Polskie Skrzydła**

[263-264]: '114' in the new scheme after major overhaul at WZL-2 Bydgoszcz (1st period). Mińsk Mazowiecki, March 2007.
[265]: Mińsk Mazowiecki, September 2008.

[266-268]: '114' with patches of new paint on the forward fuselage, near the nose radome and on forward portions of the wings.
[266, 228]: Poznań-Krzesiny, May 2008, [267] Mińsk Mazowiecki, January 2009.

83

Polish Wings

NO. 114 | MiG-29

[269]

[270]

[269]: '114' in flight above clouds, August 2009. The machine received a commemorative inscription on the 20th anniversary of the MiG-29's entry into service with the Polish Air Force.
[270]: The commemorative inscription applied by ground crew of the 1. elt: "1989-2009 20th anniversary of the MiG-29 in POLAND".
[271-274]: Parts of '114' with clearly visible patches of new paint. Mińsk Mazowiecki. August 2009.

[271]

[272]

[273]

[274]

84

NO. 115 | MiG-29   **Polskie Skrzydła**

[275]: '115' in the factory applied camouflage (Russian delivery) scheme. The machine has the 'Mermaid' badge of the 1. PLM on both sides of the fuselage. Poznań-Krzesiny, 1991.

[276, 277]: Still in the factory (Russian delivery) scheme, with a large badge of the French 2^e Escadre from Dijon-Longvic on the upper surface of the fuselage. French colours and a small badge of the 2^e Escadre were also applied on the vertical tail. The aircraft has the 'Mermaid' badge of the 1. PLM on both sides of the fuselage. Mińsk Mazowiecki, October 1994.

Polish Wings

NO. 115 | MiG-29

278 MiG-29 no. 296053515, '115' of the 1. PLM, Mińsk Mazowiecki, 1994. Aircraft in the Russian delivery scheme with additional markings.

NO. 115 | MiG-29   **Polskie Skrzydła**

[279-281]: '115' still in the special scheme, during pre-flight preparations at Mińsk Mazowiecki. May 1996.

Polish Wings

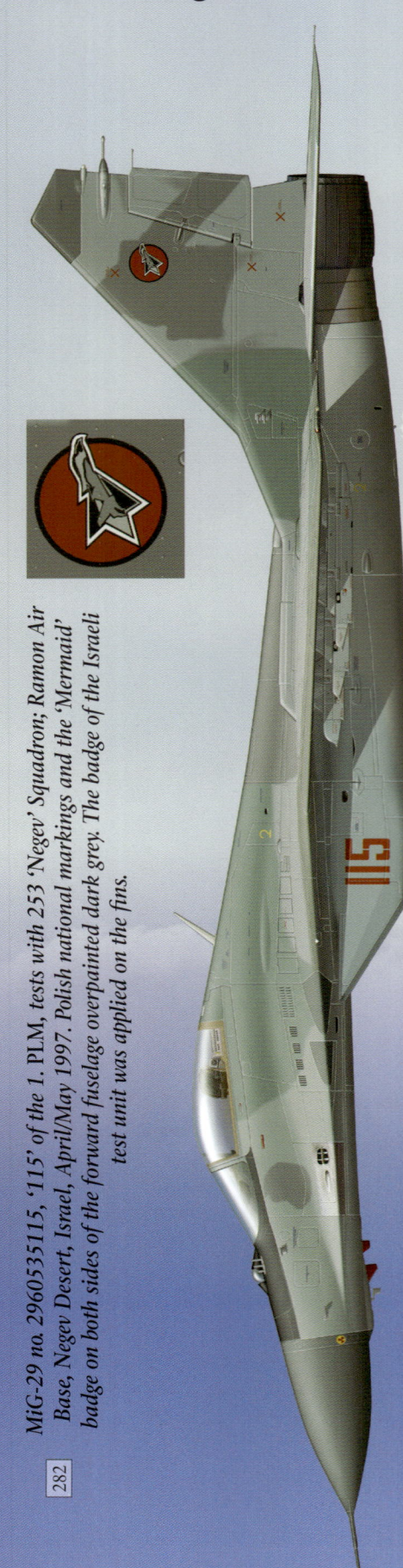

NO. 115 | MiG-29

[282] MiG-29 no. 296053S115, '115' of the 1. PLM, tests with 253 'Negev' Squadron; Ramon Air Base, Negev Desert, Israel, April/May 1997. Polish national markings and the 'Mermaid' badge on both sides of the forward fuselage overpainted dark grey. The badge of the Israeli test unit was applied on the fins.

[283]: Dęblin, August 1998. Upon return from Israel Polish markings were reapplied, as was the 'Mermaid' badge on both sides of the forward fuselage. The aircraft shows numerous patches of new paint on wing edges and upper surfaces, on wing-fuselage joints, vertical tails and around the cockpit.

[284]: '115' in flight at high altitude. Patches of new paint can be seen on the wings and the overpainted French badge on the fuselage shows through as the coat of paint has peeled off. The aircraft has a new nose radome with patches of new paint on it.

NO. 115 | MiG-29

Polskie Skrzydła

MiG-29 no. 296053515, '115' of the 1. elt, Mińsk Mazowiecki, 2002. Aircraft with the special markings overpainted.

285

Polish Wings

NO. 115 | MiG-29

[286, 287]: '115' taxiing at Mińsk Mazowiecki in April 2006, after its first major overhaul at WZL-2 Bydgoszcz (1st period). Upon return to the 1. elt the 'Mermaid' badge was not reapplied, but the Kościuszko badge was painted under the cockpit on the port side. Mińsk Mazowiecki, April 2006 [286], October 2005 [287].

[289] The emblem is applied on both fins. The personal motif of a four-leaf clover is applied on both sides of the fuselage aft of the cockpit and the Kościuszko badge is on the port side under the cockpit. Eyes were applied on the air intake covers. For the AF unit commanders' fly-in in May 2006 the rank, name and nickname of the 1. elt commander was applied under the cockpit: 'ppłk dypl. pil. R. CIERNIAK c/s „SKUTER"'.

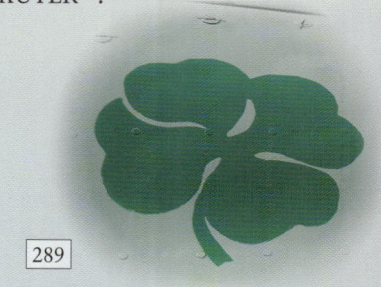

[288]: Ppłk dypl. Robert Cierniak in the cockpit of '115' with his name and personal emblem as applied during the aircraft's deployment to Lithuania, 8 May 2006.

NO. 115 | MiG-29

Polskie Skrzydła

MiG-29 no. 2960535115, '115' of pptk. pil. Robert 'Skuter' Cierniak, 1. elt, Mińsk Mazowiecki, 2008. Aircraft with post-overhaul scheme (1st period) with individual markings.

290

91

Polish Wings

NO. 115 | MiG-29

[291]: '115' taxiing at Mińsk Mazowiecki, March 2007.

[292]: '115' in the post-overhaul scheme with the PKW 'Orlik' emblem on the fin. In July 2008 the entire nose part of the fuselage was repainted, and both the clover personal motif and the Kościuszko badge were obliterated. The machine was flown without any emblems until July 2008. The eye motifs on the air intakes were retained.

NO. 115 | MiG-29

Polskie Skrzydła

[293]: '115' in the altered scheme with the forward fuselage repainted. The emblem of the PKW 'Orlik' on the fins and the eyes on the air intake covers were retained. During late July the aircraft received the 'Mermaid' badge on the starboard side of the fuselage (facing backwards). Mińsk Mazowiecki, August 2008.

[294]

Polish Wings

Polskie Skrzydła

[295]: Main instrument panel of a MiG-29 with the HUD visible.
[296-297]: Cockpit of MiG-29 '89'. Photos were taken in 2004.

Polish Wings

[298]: Port side of the cockpit of '89' with the throttle.
[299]: E-50 direct current switchboard.